WRITE & SPEAK
LIKE A
PROFESSIONAL

Other Titles of Interest from LearningExpress

Manage Your Time & Your Life in 20 Minutes a Day

WRITE & SPEAK LIKE A PROFESSIONAL

In 20 Minutes
A Day

MIRIAM SALPETER

LEARNINGEXPRESS ®

NEW YORK

Copyright © 2016 LearningExpress

All rights reserved under International and Pan American Copyright Conventions.
Published in the United States by LearningExpress, New York.

Library of Congress Cataloging-in-Publication Data: On file

ISBN: 978-1-61103-055-6
Printed in the United States of America

9 8 7 6 5 4 3 2 1

For more information or to place an order, contact LearningExpress at:
224 W. 29th Street
3rd floor
New York, NY 10001

CONTENTS ▶

CONTENTS

CONTENTS

CONTENTS

CONTENTS

About the Author

Miriam Salpeter is a social media strategist, job search coach, speaker, author, and founder of Keppie Careers (www.keppiecareers.com), a consultancy serving businesses and job seekers. Forbes named Miriam's blog a "best career resource" and CNN called her a "top 10 job tweeter you should be following." Top media outlets, including *The Wall Street Journal, The New York Times, Business Insider,* and others recognize Miriam as an expert resource for job seekers and entrepreneurs.

Author of *Social Networking for Career Success* (in its second edition*)* and *Manage Your Time & Life in 20 Minutes a Day,* and co-author of *100 Conversations for Career Success* and *Social Networking for Business Success,* Miriam is well known as a go-to expert and consultant regarding job search and social media strategies.

"In addition to coaching job seekers and small business owners, Miriam is an in-demand writer, speaker, and trainer for groups and organizations. She authors articles for company blogs and teaches job seekers and employees how to use social media. Miriam also runs "The Smart Business Owner's Social Media Help Desk," an online program to teach business owners how to leverage social media marketing tools. She authors online bios and job search materials for clients at every level of their careers.

With a BA in Honors English from the University of Michigan,

Miriam launched her career with a Wall Street firm. She left as a vice president to earn a master's degree from Columbia University with a focus on career guidance. Miriam headed the Career Action Center at the Rollins School of Public Health of Emory University before launching Keppie Careers. She has been empowering job seekers and small business owners since 2003.

Miriam lives in Atlanta with her husband, Mike, their three boys, two cats, and two rescue dogs. She invites you to connect with her on Twitter @Keppie_Careers and to touch base via her blog.

Introduction

Everyone you meet will form opinions about you based on what you say and write. Strong written and spoken communication skills are crucial to opening doors. Research by Millennial Branding has showed that soft skills top the list of "must have" skills that employers want, with 98 percent of employers saying communication skills are essential.

It's up to you to make the most of every opportunity to prove you're capable and confident. It's no secret that first impressions matter—that's been the case since the beginning of time. What's new in our increasingly fast-paced, digitally connected world, is how a simple stroke of a keyboard, or an email gone awry, can quickly damage a professional reputation. On the other hand, a stream of consistent, well-written social media updates can just as easily raise your profile and impress people you've never met, who may positively influence your career.

As a job search coach and social media strategist experienced at helping job seekers and business owners market themselves online and in person, it's clear to me that the most successful professionals make an effort to improve their communication skills at every opportunity. Whether your focus is networking, job searching, or excelling at work, it's more important now than ever to know how to present yourself in person and in writing in this hyper-competitive work environment.

Write & Speak Like a Professional in 20 Minutes a Day provides instructions and exercises to improve your communication abilities and offers insights and ideas to help refine your skills in every aspect of your job or career. It includes guidance on everything from networking to resume writing and interviewing. Communication skills are just as important in the workplace as they are when looking for a job, so you'll also find details about how to impress people at work and how to write clear, concise professional emails that will get the best results. With attention spans growing shorter, it's never been more important to learn how to hone in on your message and eliminate non-crucial details. Use this book to recognize if you're missing opportunities to communicate succinctly and learn how to remedy any problems.

Whether you're attending a meeting or writing a memo, it's up to you to put your best foot forward. This book provides resources to help you identify any deficiencies or problems you may not have considered. For example, are you using words in your emails that call your professionalism into question? Does the tone or inflection of your voice make people think you aren't confident? Could you be doing more via social media to expand your reach and extend your influence in your professional community? How are your listening skills? Does your body language send the message you want people to receive?

Read on to learn how to improve your ability to make a strong first impression, and how to extend and enhance that impression so your colleagues and supervisors will listen carefully when you speak, and appreciate what you write.

WRITE & SPEAK LIKE A PROFESSIONAL

I NETWORKING

Communicate Professionally When Networking in Person

1

People will determine if you're credible, qualified, and capable based on their first impressions of you. That's a lot of pressure, but luckily, you do have control over how you come across. With advance planning, in-person networking can help you improve your professional standing. Don't approach networking events casually, as you would any other in-person gathering; you'll miss out on opportunities as a result. Read on to learn the most successful way to prepare yourself so that you make a solid impression at in-person networking events.

Plan What to Say: Pay Attention to the World Around You!

Do you get wrapped up in your own life and forget to pay attention to what's going on in the world? It's much easier to make small talk with strangers when you're familiar with current events. Before you attend a networking event, make a point to watch, read, or listen to the news. Pay special attention to major events that capture the public's attention, including sports, entertainment, and politics. If you know what topics interest people you will meet, you're less likely to feel awkward and out-of-place when the conversation turns to the hottest television show or athletes in the news. While politics may not be the wisest choice for professional networking conversations, it's useful to be aware of political events or personalities so you won't appear clueless if the conversation takes a turn in that direction.

GOOD RESOURCES TO KEEP ON TOP OF THE NEWS OF THE DAY

No matter what your field or profession, keep up with your professional and general interest topics and news. With all the online tools available at the touch of your smartphone, there's no excuse for not knowing what is going on in any interest area. Here are some good resources to get started:

- **SmartBrief.com:** For work related news in any number of fields, including marketing, healthcare, social media, and other topics, you can rely on free SmartBrief newsletters, delivered directly to your email.
- **AllTop.com:** For general interest news on any topic imaginable, from baseball to x-rays, check out AllTop.com, a list of blogs categorized by interest type.
- **ZeeBox:** If you want to keep up with the latest television news, this app keeps you abreast of the buzz and allows you to chat with other viewers.
- **Goodreads:** If you want to seem in touch with what everyone is reading, you can find book reviews and share your thoughts about what you are reading.

continued from page 2

- **Flipboard:** A news aggregator that provides a collection of magazine-like links to Facebook, Twitter, and other sites, based on your interest choices.
- **LinkedIn Pulse:** Part of LinkedIn, this app allows you to pull in your choice of online information sources and creates magazine-like pages with thumbnail photos and headlines from different sources.
- **ESPN:** Keep up with a variety of sports via this app, which even lets you stream sports on television.

How to prepare in advance

In our book *100 Conversations for Career Success*, Laura Labovich and I suggested the following steps to be sure you're prepared to be a great conversationalist at networking events:

1. List topics you enjoy discussing and would be comfortable bringing up in networking conversations. List at least five things you're an expert at or you enjoy. Consider including items such as sports, movies, books, and news events in your list.
2. List some current books, movies, and magazines you intend to learn about before you attend your next networking meeting.
3. Visit several of the resources and apps suggested in this book to keep up-to-date with topics of interest to you.
4. Make a list of questions to engage new contacts. Include a list of open-ended inquiries. These questions require an in-depth reply and can't be answered with a simple "yes" or "no." They often start with who, what, when, where, and why. For example:

   - *How did you find out about this group?*
   - *What do you like most about this organization?*

- *How did you get started doing that work?*
- *Who is your favorite _____ (insert something that relates to your industry or field)?*

Exercise: List some open-ended questions that would make sense for contacts specific to your industry. Don't forget to start them with who, what, when, where, and why.

1. _____

2. _____

3. _____

4. _____

5. _____

Identify What You Offer

Everyone knows someone who always seems to have just the right bit of information at the right time. If you need a name of a restaurant for a first date, this person has the perfect suggestion. You want the name of an electrician to fix something in your new home? He knows just who to call. These people are connectors. They connect other people to information. Everyone has the potential to be a connector.

Lynn Wong, a senior director in global logistics at a Fortune 500 company, suggests the best networkers identify touch points that connect all of us—but don't necessarily have anything to do with work. Focus on what you have to give. Her suggestions:

- Food connects people—where can you get the best wings in town? What's your favorite recipe?

- Sports—where can you go to play tennis that isn't crowded?
- Where to get tickets for events.
- Favorite vacation spots.
- Online resources for finding great sales, learning what's new in the area, or finding a plumber.

Exercise: What are some of *your* areas of expertise? Make a note of the topics you love to discuss, and use them as jumping off points when doing research in advance of attending an event.

I especially enjoy when the topic of conversation includes:

1. _____

2. _____

3. _____

4. _____

5. _____

Some resources for me to learn more about these topics include:

1. _____

2. _____

3. _____

4. _____

5. _____

Research Who Will Attend

It's a lot easier to be prepared for great conversations when you know whom you can expect to meet. Even personal events, such as birthday party invitations, often come via email with online RSVPs that make it easy to see who's attending. Facebook and other online tools offer easy ways to click through to learn more about who might attend a party or program. Don't stop with a list of potential attendees; use the resources available to you to learn as much as you can about key people you want to meet.

Identify people who may be good contacts for you, and find out more about them. If you don't know anyone on the list, consider it an opportunity to expand your network. Google their names to help determine their backgrounds and interests. Use LinkedIn to easily identify where people work, their alma maters, and even their volunteer interests. Don't forget to enlist friends during your research—ask people you trust for names of people who plan to attend the event, and learn what you can about their backgrounds.

Exercise: Every time you attend a networking event, be sure to perform the following exercises. It's time well-spent!

List information you want to find out about people who will attend the event.

1. _____

2. _____

3. _____

4. _____

5. _____

Make a chart of the info you discover:

Name	Profession	Company	University	Interests	Questions to Ask

Make Introductions

Introductions are very important when it comes to in-person networking. Learn to confidently introduce yourself and to introduce two people to each other, and you'll be well prepared to expand your network.

How to introduce yourself

What should you say when someone asks you, "Tell me about yourself?" This is a deceptively simple inquiry that isn't really so simple. Your goal during an introduction is to inspire interest—not boredom.

The key to a successful introduction: forget everything you learned about a "two-minute elevator pitch." No one is going to listen to you drone on for two minutes! If you can't say who you are and what you do in 35 words or less, assume people will stop listening. If you want to be really succinct, create a micro pitch of 140 characters or less, about the length of a tweet.

ANSWER THESE QUESTIONS IN YOUR PITCH:

- What do you do?
- What do you offer?
- What makes you special and unique? (Relative to the person you're meeting.)
- What is your goal/objective?
- What do you WANT to do?
- What impact do you have?
- What results do you create?
- How do you create positive results?
- Why should your audience care? (Target your pitch so it's relevant to each person you meet.)

Use this template to create your pitch. Note that the information doesn't need to be in this exact order:

I work with [*target audience*].
To [*situation/solve what problem*].
This is how [*results/impact*].

Here's a sample pitch for me and my company, Keppie Careers:

As an author, speaker, and coach, I help job seekers and small business owners achieve their goals by writing resumes and marketing materials, and by teaching them how to leverage the power of social networks. (35 words)

Exercise: What's your short pitch?

_____

_____

_____

_____

_____

_____

What to say when you first meet

Once you've researched topics to discuss, learned a bit about the people you'll meet, and filled in your chart with this information, it will be much easier to start a conversation with the potential to grow a relationship with new contacts. (It's not a bad idea to keep a few notes about the people you've researched in your smartphone, or even on a few index cards.)

Think about how you can help the people you want to meet. What interesting information can you offer? For example, perhaps you've learned one of your target contacts attended your alma mater, and you're a member of the local alumni association. Or, you read a food blog one of your contacts writes. If you're a foodie, you have an immediate point of contact.

How can you get started? Consider taking the role of the person who introduces others at the event. Typically, attendees will wear nametags. Step outside of your comfort zone and play "host." Find two people and act like it's your party—introduce them to each other. Ask what brings them there and ask questions about themselves. (Feel free to bring up your key touch points you like to talk about.)

How to introduce someone else

The best part of introducing people to each other? Once you've introduced someone to another person, that person will be more compelled to introduce *you* to someone else.

Scenario

A few people are standing around. You approach one of the women:

You (to the woman you don't know, while viewing her name tag):
Hello, Marge, I'm Sue. Can you believe this weather?
Marge: *Yes, it has been so cold lately.*
You: *I'm glad they have hot coffee here! Are you a member of this organization?*
Marge: *No, I am new.*
You: *Me, too. This is my first time here.* [Looking at the other person's nametag] *Jenny, do you know Marge? Marge, this is Jenny. Have you been to one of these meetings before?*

You can see how easy it is to be a connector and introduce two people to each other, even if you didn't know either one of them.

What to say when you are re-introduced

It is awkward to respond when someone re-introduces you to someone you already know. It's even worse when they don't remember you already met. Be casual and take it in stride if someone doesn't remember you. For example, you may say, "I think we might have met at the XYZ event back in January? At the wine tasting?" If the person still doesn't remember you, simply note how nice it is to meet and don't dwell on his or her faux pas.

How to Make a Break for It

One of the most challenging things about a networking event is when you're cornered by the most talkative person in the room, the person who hasn't read this book about professional communication and doesn't realize you're only being polite by continuing to stand beside him! Actually, you stopped listening to what he was saying 20 minutes ago.

How can you save yourself? You have a few choices:

- *It's been so nice to speak with you. Can we exchange contact information?*
- *Thanks for sharing some of your stories with me. I need to check in with the office. It was nice to meet you.*
- *I'm going to pick up a piece of that cheesecake. Can I get you something?* (Usually, the person will decline, and you're free.)

Follow Up

Luckily, there will be many networking contacts with whom you'll want to maintain contact. Following up is *your* job. Don't count on your new contacts to keep in touch, especially if you have more to gain from the relationship than they do.

Most importantly, *do* follow up. If you say you're going to be in touch, and you don't follow up, that isn't very compelling.

Follow up in writing

Since snail mail isn't common anymore, sending a written (or typed) note will often help you stand out from a crowd. If you want to see someone again, be sure to include details from your meeting to make sure the person remembers your initial encounter. Jot some items down when you meet people so you'll know what to say when you send your follow-up note. Be careful to ensure your letter doesn't include any typos or other errors. If you hand write the note, be sure it is legible.

Use the following as an example when taking notes and creating a final letter:

Name of person: Josiah Ross

What he/she was wearing/appearance note: Red striped tie, tall, black hair, and blue glasses

What I was wearing: Orange dress and blue scarf

What we discussed: Jo owns a consulting firm and needs some help with web design

Key "remember" point: I offered to provide a free assessment of his site and suggestions for improvements

Follow-up action: Best to call between 9 and 3 p.m./ 555-555-5555

Dear Josiah,

It was great meeting you last night at the opening of The Sizzling Grill Restaurant. I'm glad we had a chance to talk about your website needs. Hopefully, you'll remember our conversation; I was the one wearing an orange dress and blue scarf. As you suggested, I will plan to give you a call next week during the day at your office number to discuss providing a free evaluation of your site. As we discussed, web design and optimization are my specialties, and I am happy to work with a fellow Atlantan.

Sincerely,

Miriam

Follow up via phone

Don't hesitate to reach someone by phone, even if you haven't sent a written note. The trick to successful communication at this stage is to be prepared for all scenarios. What if your contact actually answers the phone, and you were expecting a receptionist? Are you prepared to launch directly into your quick pitch? On the other hand, be prepared if it's your fifth time calling, and you get the answering machine. You don't want to leave a rambling message; plan ahead so you'll know what to say.

Handling Gatekeepers

If a gatekeeper answers the phone, be ready to give a good reason to pass along a message: "I met Ms. Jones at the Marketers of America event last night, and she suggested I get in touch to arrange a meeting." (This is a great opening line only if it is true!) Alternatively, you may say you are working on a project and wish to include her insights. If you don't think you're getting what you need, you can always request to be transferred to voice mail.

If the same receptionist picks up the phone every time you call for your target contact, you can sometimes win favor by being attentive to his or her needs and being very polite and accommodating. Convince the gatekeeper to be your ally. Never sound annoyed or disappointed or take out your frustration on the gatekeeper, who is just doing his or her job.

A simple inquiry, for example, "I wonder if you'd be willing to help me?" can go a long way. Get the gatekeeper's name and make a point to convince that person to provide useful information for you. You may say, "I hate to keep bothering you...can you tell me a good time to reach Ms. Jones?"

Timing is Everything

Ideally, you've asked for and listed the best time to try to reach the person in your notes. If not, you may want to try to place your call first thing in the morning or later in the day—but not too late in the day.

Consider the scenario: it's the end of a busy day, and your contact is anxiously finishing things before leaving for the evening. You call. What are the chances of getting through to someone not expecting to hear from you? Morning is usually a better time than evening, but if you can learn something about the person's schedule, you'll be more likely to reach him or her. If your target contact uses social media, you can try to see if anything posted there may help you. For example, if he's traveling or at an event, you'll want to time your call for another day.

What to Say When You Reach Your Contact

Don't spend too much time with small talk; get to the point. No one really cares about the weather; you probably have two or three sentences worth of talking before the person decides if you are worth more time or not. This is your pitch. Use those words well. What can you say? Focus on what you can do for the person, not what you want him or her to do for you.

Leave a Compelling Voicemail Message

Keep your notes in front of you when you call, and consider writing a script of what you want to say. Don't assume the person will or will not answer—be prepared for all scenarios, and know what you'll say. Use the same information you used (or would have used) in your written follow up. Remember to mention when and where you met, provide details to help the person remember you (such as what you wore or discussed), and provide details about how you can help. Be sure to be polite, no matter how the person responds to your call.

Say something compelling to pique the person's interest. For example, you may indicate you have information you'd like to share about a particular issue you know the individual is facing, or you can say you're seeking the contact's expertise for a project.

Follow up via social media

Sometimes, the best way to follow up is via social media channels. Always remember to ask new contacts if you can send them an invitation to connect via LinkedIn. Be sure to send the invitation directly from the person's LinkedIn page so you can personalize your invite, and avoid sending LinkedIn's canned invitation. You can only include a short note, but include as much of the same information as you might have sent in your written message. It's important to remind the person when and where you met, in case your new contact sees your message in a week or two and doesn't remember you.

If you and your new contact both use other social networks such as Twitter, you can try to reconnect with him or her using those channels. Be sure to include the person's username for that network in your message. For example:

> *@NewContact: it was great to meet at XYZ meeting last night. Will follow up re: website evaluation.*

Learn more about how to use social media professionally in Chapter 4.

In Summary: Action Tips

Networking well is crucial to your professional success. First impressions matter, and it's your job to influence what people think of you. Be prepared and you'll expand your networking options.

Here are some actionable items to prepare for any networking event:

- Plan ahead. Research and prepare so you'll have several great topics in mind to discuss. Do your best to learn who will be in attendance. Learn something about your go-to networking contacts.
- Practice what you'll say when you meet new people. Consider your expertise and what advice people would appreciate. Know what you have to offer and leverage it when you network. Be generous with information and resources.
- Prepare to introduce yourself and be able to easily answer the question, "Tell me about yourself." Keep it short and focus on what the person wants to know. Answer these questions:

  - What do you do? What do you offer? What makes you special and unique? (Relative to the person you're meeting.)
  - What is your goal/objective? What do you WANT to do?
  - What impact do you have? What results do you create?
  - How do you create positive results?
  - Why should the person care? (Target your pitch so it's relevant to each person you meet.)

Use this template to create your pitch.

I work with [*target audience*].

To [*situation/solve what problem*].

This is how [*results/impact*].

Once you're comfortable introducing yourself, plan to introduce other people to each other. Once you've introduced someone to another person, that person will be more compelled to introduce you to someone else.

- **Find out a little personal information about new contacts.** Ask where they vacation, about their family, and their hobbies.
- **Always follow up with contacts you want to see again.** Use email or the phone, and don't forget to send links and newsworthy articles.
- **Plan when to call or write.** Keep in mind that timing is important when following up. Don't call at the end of the day, and be prepared to convince gatekeepers that you're an important call to put through.
- **Use social media tools.** Don't forget social media can be a good way to touch base with a new networking contact and to remind someone of you

2 Make a Positive Impression in Your Writing

Written communication is just as crucial to your professional reputation as your in-person interactions. An otherwise well-written message or memo to your department or boss can become a credibility killer due to one ill-placed typo if you aren't careful.

Be Professional

It's easy to fall into the trap of sending a quick email in "text speak," with words shortened and spelling ignored. Avoid this. While email may seem like a casual medium, everything your put in writing forms a foundation of what people will think about you. Consider everything you write, whether it's an email, printed note, memo, or letter, as if you were editing and publishing a newspaper for wide circulation. Be careful what you write, as every item may influence your professional potential.

Pay Attention to Spelling, Grammar, and Syntax

Since written communication can be saved for posterity and easily forwarded on to other contacts or colleagues, it's especially important to be careful with grammar and syntax (how you place words in sentences). The best way to help improve your writing is to read a lot—everything from well-written literature to news and magazines from well-regarded publishers. Newspapers with national reputations are good choices, such as *The New York Times* or *Washington Post*. You can find a lot of well-written content online, so there is no excuse to not read.

Another way to improve your writing is to practice writing. If you know your writing could use a lot of work, consider taking a class or joining a writing group. Having other people read, edit, and critique your writing can really help you fix bad habits and learn better writing strategies. Be honest with yourself and seek outside help if you are not proud of how you write.

Keep these tips in mind to help improve your writing.

Plan ahead

You can't communicate well until you know what you want to say. Determine your main idea and outline everything around it before you start to compose something important.

Whether you're composing an email that will be read by higher-ups at your company or a cover letter responding to your dream job, answer these questions first—they'll really help your writing take shape and will ensure it covers everything you want to say.

What is my main message?

_____

_____

_____

What does my audience need to know after they read this message?

_____

_____

_____

What action do I want my audience to take?

_____

_____

_____

What words will resonate most with my audience? (For example, if you plan to use lingo or acronyms, be sure the audience will understand them.)

_____

_____

_____

Answer these questions and your writing is sure to be targeted and to the point.

Keep it simple

It's very easy to lose your credibility when you try to use words you don't really understand. While you do want to expand your vocabulary, don't use complex language unnecessarily in writing. When you do, you may appear clueless (at best) and ignorant (at worst).

Don't string too much together

Run-on sentences are a common writing error. Don't try to put too much into one thought or sentence. Consider how you could simplify your sentences so they include one subject and one main idea.

Avoid misspelled words

While most writers use spell check tools or other technology when writing, don't rely on these digital editors. Pay careful attention to words spell check tools won't correct, such as *manger* instead of *manager* or *pubic* instead of *public*. Google {commonly misspelled words} for online lists to review and learn how to spell words you may be writing incorrectly. Be careful not to mistake common homophones (words that sound alike but are spelled differently). It can be a real credibility killer when you send professional correspondence with these mistakes.

Commonly misspelled words

These are some of the most commonly misused words:

- *To* and *too.* To means toward. For example, "I am going to the bank." Too can mean in addition, such as "So smart, and pretty, too." It also indicates excessive. For example, "Don't eat too much cake."

- *Its* and *it's.* Use the contraction rule to check it's. Replace your choice with it is. If that does not make sense, its is correct. Its indicates possession. "The bowl doesn't have its lid." On the other hand, if it is works, you would choose the contraction, "It's getting very late."

- *Your* and *you're.* This is an easy one if you replace you're with the words you are. If you are does not make sense, you should use your instead, which indicates possession. The correct use: "You're going to appreciate your brother when you are older."

- *There, their,* and *they're.* Contractions are always easy to check, because you can replace them with the words they suggest. If "they are" does not fit in your sentence, do not use they're. There indicates a place. For example, "We will be going there in two weeks." Their indicates possession, as if someone owns something. Here's a sentence that uses all three: "They're so crazy about their cat, they take her over there all the time."

There are many other commonly misused words, but if you correct these, you'll avoid a lot of common errors.

Always edit your writing

You can save yourself a lot of grief and aggravation by simply reading over your writing before you send it. If possible, try to put aside what you write for at least a few hours (overnight is better) before you review or edit it. Read it out loud to yourself or to a friend. You may want to increase the font size and print it out to read if you usually edit on the computer screen. Another trick is to read each word individually. In addition, consider reviewing your writing backwards. These techniques all help you catch silly mistakes.

Look for words you can delete

Always consider the reader. He or she is likely looking at your message while simultaneously doing one or more other things. Make sure your message isn't so complex that it overshadows the point. If you over-repeat the point, cull it down so your message is shorter.

Words that Damage Credibility

Especially in written communication, when people can easily review your message more than once, each word packs an extra punch—either positive or negative. Consider how these choices may negatively affect your credibility.

In an article for *The Muse*, Lily Herman, Founder of Theprospect. net, mentions several words to eliminate from your correspondence:

Hopefully

"*Hopefully*, you'll have a chance to get back to me." This word can be interpreted as sounding a little desperate. Leave it off and see how your email reads without it.

Actually

Who would think one little adverb could call your credibility into question? However, if you respond to an email saying, "*Actually*, I believe we should choose option 1," you're including a word with no specific value. Avoid it. Herman says, "*Actually* is slowly becoming the new '*literally*' or '*basically*' in emails." In other words, it's an extra word that doesn't necessarily fit in the context of the message. Read through your messages and make sure you aren't overusing this (or another) unnecessary word that detracts from your message. In addition, including *actually* may give your email a scolding tone, as if you're correcting someone else's information. For example, "Actually, that meeting is on Monday, not Tuesday" sounds negative. A better way to communicate the information would be to state, "I have the meeting on my calendar for Monday. I look forward to seeing you at 10 a.m."

Kind of

Herman notes, similar to *sort of*, this phrase is vague and not useful.

Sorry

Is it really necessary to apologize? If you haven't done anything wrong, there's no need to say *sorry* in your emails.

Sujan Patel, VP of Marketing for *When I Work*, added a few other phrases to avoid in an article for *Inc*. His suggestions included:

Please be advised

While it sounds official and professional, it's better to just get to the point in your message.

Please do not hesitate to contact me

Patel notes that you're stating the obvious when you use this phrase. If they want to contact you, they will.

I think

It's obvious that you think so, or you would not make the point in your message.

I thought I would reach out

Patel explains that this is a timid phrase, not appropriate for professional communication.

Can I pick your brain?

This unappealing visual suggests you want something from the contact person and indicates you have nothing to give in return. It's not a good way to ask for advice.

Words that hedge

In an article for *Business Insider*, Sarah Schmalbruch interviewed Deborah Tannen, author of *Talking From 9 To 5: Women and Men at Work* and a professor of linguistics at Georgetown University. She listed words and phrases such as *sort of*, *kind of*, *pretty much*, and *maybe* as indicators you aren't confident of what you're communicating. Evaluate your writing for these and avoid introducing doubt about your abilities.

Intensifiers

Schmalbruch's article listed *really*, *definitely*, *absolutely*, and *totally*, which she labeled *intensifers*, words to avoid because, when used, they have the opposite of their intended effect. In other words, if you are *definitely* interested in everything (in other words, you overuse the word), it takes away from the meaning. Avoid sounding over-the-top when you communicate and you'll have more credibility.

So

Writing for *Fast Company*, Hunter Thurman, founder of the consultancy, Thriveplan, and author of *Brand Be Nimble*, writes that beginning a sentence with *so* indicates you're trying to dumb down what you say next and undermines your credibility, as it suggests you are not completely comfortable with what you are saying. Thurman explains that the word *so* acts as a marker. He explains it's a "cue that says, 'Quick, call up that part that we practiced.'" Avoid it and earn more credibility.

Probably and try

In another article for *The Muse*, Lily Herman notes several words that don't inspire a lot of trust. *Probably* (or, its close cousin *hopefully*) suggests you are not very confident. Similarly, if you're going to *try* to do something, it seems likely you will not get it done.

Think

Herman included this in her list of words to avoid in professional communication because it's unnecessary. You don't need to say "I *think*," it's obvious you do, otherwise you wouldn't be saying it. Try to drop "I *think*" from the beginnings of your sentences and see how much more powerful they read.

Honestly

Another in Herman's list for *The Muse*, this is another credibility killer. When you say *honestly*, it begs the question of what isn't honest in your note. Avoid this one, too.

I

A small word, but when overused, especially in writing but also in speaking, makes you appear overly self-centered and me focused. Even when you're writing about yourself, review your document or letter for the word *I* and try to revise the text so it is not so self-referential.

Just

Ellen Petry Leanse, a former Google executive and entrepreneur, made an interesting observation about a word she believes negatively affects credibility, both in writing and speaking. She observed that the word *just* inserted in written and verbal communication can be interpreted as a "subtle message of subordination," and as deferential, self-effacing, or even duplicitous. Her examples include:

> *I just wanted to check in on...*
> *Just wondering if you'd decided between...*
> *If you can just give me an answer, then...*
> *I'm just following up on...*

Consider how you're changing the tone of your message when you incorporate *if* in your written (and verbal) communication.

The Passive Voice

While not technically a grammatical error, your writing will be more powerful if you avoid the passive voice. Except for scientific writing, which makes use of the passive voice, you're better off avoiding this structure.

An example of a passive sentence structure:
The boy was hit by the door.

An edited, non-passive voice version:
The door hit the boy.

The passive voice is often used by people who want to avoid giving people credit or assigning blame. For example, *mistakes were made* is passive. To make this sentence active, you need to know who made these mistakes, "Susan made mistakes" or "the team made mistakes" would be active examples.

THE PASSIVE VOICE TEST

A good test for the passive voice is to see if you could add the phrase *by zombies* to your sentence. If you can, it is passive. For example, "Mistakes were made...*by zombies*." Or, "The boy was hit....*by zombies*." "The printer was broken...*by zombies*."

Exercise: Answer **True** or **False**.

_____ **1.** One ill-placed typo in an email is not the end of the world. You don't need to worry about how it will affect people's opinions of you and your attention to detail.

_____ **2.** Reading well-written literature (such as classics) as well as news and magazines from well-regarded publishers isn't a very good idea, because it will encourage you to be too intellectual with your writing.

_____ **3.** *To* means *in addition*, such as "So smart, and pretty, *to*." It also indicates *excessive*. For example, "Don't eat *to* much cake."

_____ **4.** *Its* indicates possession. For example, "The bowl doesn't have *its* lid."

_____ **5.** Flowery language makes you seem smart and professional.

_____ **6.** Words or phrases that hedge (*sort of, kind of*) make you sound humble and will attract others.

_____ **7.** There is always room in your writing for the word *so*, especially for those who like to informally tell a good story.

_____ **8.** Reading your writing out loud to yourself or to a friend, or increasing the font size, are good ideas when editing.

_____ **9.** You should always say "*I think*" when you're giving an opinion.

_____ **10.** Passive voice means you're talking about something that already happened.

Answers

1. **F.** One typo can negatively affect what people think of your professionalism.

2. **F.** The more you read, including strong writing samples, the better your grammar and syntax become.

3. **F.** To means *toward*.

4. **T.** *Its* indicates possession. *It's* means *it is*.

5. **F.** Flowery, excessive language makes you appear unsure of yourself and encourages you to use words you may not understand. Avoid it and be direct.

6. **F.** These words make you sound unsure of yourself and of what you know. That doesn't inspire confidence.

7. **F.** *So* is not a very professional word choice. Try to avoid it.

8. **T.** This can help catch mistakes.

9. **F.** Avoid using *I think* in your writing. It is clear what you write is your opinion.

10. **F.** Passive voice is a tool writers employ when they don't want to assign blame. Otherwise, avoid it.

In Summary: Action Tips

You'll always want to create the most professional content possible when you communicate in writing. Keep these action items in mind and you'll avoid the trap of communicating too informally at work.

- Pay attention to spelling, grammar, and syntax in all of your writing. Pay special attention to commonly misused words, such as *to* and *too* or *its* and *it's*.
- Plan what you write, to be sure you focus on one digestible message.
- Edit your writing before you send it, to avoid errors.
- Be aware of words that may damage your credibility and avoid them.
- Avoid the passive voice. Even though it's technically grammatical (and expected in scientific writing), it's more powerful to write in the active voice.

3 Communicate Professionally in Email

Writing well via email is crucial to your professional success. When you communicate in person it's easier for others to overlook or wave aside grammatical or other errors. However, when you put something in writing, it's likely your audience will re-review and evaluate it. People may forget exactly what you say to them, but they can easily ruminate over what you write. This can work in your favor if your correspondence is professional and on target. However, it can derail your professional reputation when you're not careful. Keep in mind: in writing, there are no second chances.

Include a Useful Email Subject Line

Everyone is busy and hurried. Your recipient may see your message via mobile phone while at a stoplight or in line at the grocery store. Unfortunately, we cannot assume attentiveness or focus on the part of anyone reading emails. As a result, it's your job to do everything you can to make it easy for the reader to receive and understand your message. One way to do that is via a specific, targeted subject line that makes the email look important to the person. "Information you requested" or "Thought you'd find this interesting" may do the trick. Keep messages on topic, focused on one subject, and short—or you may find the secondary issue lost in the mix.

Best subject lines for emails

No matter the situation—whether you've met a person and are following up or writing to a new contact—your subject line is crucial. Most people receive a lot more email than they ever plan to read, so strive to attract your target audience's attention—so they will read your message instead of ignoring or deleting it.

If you've ever signed up for an online email list, you've likely seen many ploys to encourage you to open the marketers' messages. For example, "Your invoice is enclosed," "Can't miss deal," or even, "Don't open this email!" All of these have their charm, but unfortunately, aren't appropriate for professional communication.

Review your own email and count how many characters appear in the subject lines. Note any differences when you review your email on your computer compared to your mobile devices. You may expect to see between 45 and 60 characters on the computer, and between 20 and 30 characters on a phone. (Assume a majority of people will read emails on their phones.) With that in mind, your best bet is to use something informational and to the point. Avoid any filler or unnecessary words—for example, "Hello." You want to lead your email with the information people need to know to decide if it's crucial enough to open.

Email subject lines for in-person meeting follow up

If you met the person at an event, consider these subjects:

- *Following up from XYZ meeting*
- *Information you requested*

- *Requesting meeting re: XYZ event*
- *XYZ event follow up*
- *Scheduling meeting*

Email subject lines for requesting meetings

If you haven't met and email is your first introduction, or you are requesting a meeting, you'll need to try a different approach. Ideally, you'll be able to make some sort of connection to the person. For example:

- *Referred by Judy Smith*
- *Recommended by Sara Bradley*
- *Jim Jones said to contact you*
- *Information about ABC for you*

Email subject lines for application emails

If you're applying for a job via email, your subject line should reflect the job and its title. If there is additional information you can add that is relevant, such as your degrees or the job description number, include that as well. For example:

- *Senior Engineer Job Application*
- *Job Application: Accountant Assistant*
- *Job Candidate: Human Resources Secretary (#12345)*
- *Job Application: John Smith MBA for Marketing Manager*

Avoid generic subjects, such as "Resume for review." Provide a searchable subject line that makes it very easy for the recipient to sort and find your email at a later time if necessary.

Creative email subject lines

If you're a creative type, you may want to try a descriptive subject that may appeal to someone who is tired of the same old subject lines.

- *Perfect fit for (Job Title/ID number)*
- *Your next great hire for (Job Title)*
- *Experienced social media marketer*
- *Results guaranteed: applying for (Job Title)*

Include a Salutation

Hey may be appropriate for your college friend, but it stands out like a sore thumb in professional communication. While the very formal, *Dear Mr. Smith* may not be typical, even in professional email, a greeting such as *Hi* or *Hey* makes you sound too casual. When you're addressing a professional contact, including a professor or someone who's not a good friend, choose formal salutations to begin your messages, emails, and other notes.

Always begin your messages with some sort of salutation, such as *Dear* _____ (this is generally preferred for formal communication) or *Hello* _____. While you may be accustomed to eliminating a salutation in favor of launching directly into your message, your reader may appreciate or expect a more formal greeting. You can never go wrong by including a formal greeting in your written communication, but it's easy to offend someone who has formal expectations by addressing them with *Hey* with no opening at all.

Replying to All

No one needs another email in their inbox. While email seems innocuous and *reply all* is convenient, don't become complacent and lazy about your email. Think carefully before you hit *reply all*, especially if the message includes confidential information, or you may later regret sharing your thoughts with everyone on the receiving end of your e-mail. Avoid forwarding a message to an entire list of people unless they absolutely must receive your reply.

Always think before sending a message to a group and ask yourself if anything in the message is appropriate for everyone on the distribution list. Then, question whether or not everyone on the list would appreciate the contents of the information: do they need to have this email? If not, change your reply to reach only the necessary recipients, and everyone will be happier.

Consider these situations and evaluate whether "Reply All" is your best choice.

Who needs to know?

Does everyone on the receiving end of the message really need to know what you have to say, for example, when your boss asks everyone on the team via email to step up to handle a particular, timely project? Reply to all if you're volunteering so no one else does extra work you are already handling. However, if you are too busy, or have three other projects on your docket and cannot pick up the extra work, there is no need to reply to all. No one else needs to know what you're doing; just reply to your boss to let her know you aren't planning to take on the project unless you hear back from her.

Thanks

If you're thanking someone, unless you must absolutely share your gratitude with an entire list, your email becomes inconsequential and annoying. Send thanks directly to the people who need to see it. Otherwise, you'll likely inspire everyone else to roll their eyes in disdain when they open your email to find it contains nothing of consequence.

Personal comments

If you're adding a personal comment to your note, don't reply to all. For example, if you're asking how a person's date went last night or commenting on a coworker's recent renovation, send it only to the person intended—not to the whole office.

Angry emails

Don't reply to all when you're angry or annoyed. Generally, it's best to avoid responding to anything in writing if you are upset, but it's even more dangerous to blanket the whole office with an email written in the heat of the moment.

Snarky messages

By the same token, do not use reply all if you are being snarky, scolding, or disrespectful. Keep in mind, anything you put in writing can and will be used against you. Sending a less-than-kind message to a whole list of people increases the chances you'll regret it later.

Tips to Remember

Be especially careful to edit and review your email before you send it. Check to be sure it has all of the correct attachments. Since most people expect a quick reply, be attentive to details; it's very easy to accidentally send a message to the wrong person, especially if your email program automatically populates email addresses.

Read everything before you reply

Especially when there's an entire email thread of messages, don't waste everyone's time replying until you've actually read what everyone already responded. When you do respond before reading other replies, you could easily confuse everyone involved, which can irritate and annoy an entire list of people

Review before you send

Not all digital communication can be retrieved once sent, so make sure you review and proofread your materials before you post them. When you're in a hurry, it's easy to make a spelling or grammar mistake. Try to avoid typos by pausing and reviewing your message.

Read it out loud (even if it's out loud in your head) before you send it to make sure you didn't leave out any words or make any errors. Spell check, but recognize spell check doesn't catch all words or mistakes.

Double check the "To" field

Don't accidentally forward an important (or possibly confidential) message to the wrong person. Luckily, it's easy to verify recipients with a simple glance at the "To" field. If you have trouble with this, consider avoiding important business correspondence from your mobile phone, as it can be a little more challenging to double check all of the specifics on a small screen.

Check your CC and BCC

While it's important to keep an eye on the "To" field, make sure you don't abuse the CC and BCC. This habit represents vestiges of an earlier time, when people "carbon copied" others on important professional correspondence. However, it's easy to overdo it when it comes to copying other people to emails. Be mindful: does the other person need to see the message? What is your purpose in "BCCing" (blind copying) another party on the email? Could the secretive copy come back to hurt you later? Think carefully before you send messages and you'll be less likely to regret them.

Be sure to include the attachment

How often do you receive a note that should include an attachment, but doesn't? It's usually followed by the "Sorry, I forgot the attachment" note, or the "It would help if I include the attachment" note. Don't be the one who needs to follow up an email with yet another email. While it's not the end of the world to forget an attachment, it's best to get it right the first time. The same goes for sending the correct attachment. You don't want to accidentally forward information to the wrong person.

Don't forward chain messages

Professional communication should never include silly or frivolous emails, and that includes anything that may even appear to be a chain letter. Tip-offs? When the subject says, "Forward this to 10 people or else…." These aren't usually well-received by your friends, either. Just don't do it.

Be direct

Even though formatting and adding headlines and bullet points may help someone get through your email or other written communication, make an effort to be precise and succinct. Avoid excess verbiage and flowery language, and eliminate words intended to make you sound fancy. Unless you're a professional comedian, avoid humor and sarcasm, since it is often lost in translation. People appreciate written communication that is direct and to the point. Ideally, readers can view the entire email without scrolling on their computers, or in a quick scroll on a mobile device.

Respond promptly

People expect an immediate response to email. If you receive a reply to a message you sent or a new message requesting information, be timely in your response, while keeping mindful of the other tips to proofread and carefully consider what you send.

Format your emails

Err on the side of more formatting than less. As noted, try to keep your emails short, but if your message is longer than a paragraph, include subheadings. Bullet points or numbered lists will help people decipher your message more easily and directly. Include space between paragraphs, and don't hesitate to break up your message into more paragraphs than you might otherwise consider, which makes it easier to read.

COMMON MISTAKES TO AVOID

Never use "text speak" in your professional written communication.
As noted in Chapter 2, even if you do happen to be texting with a contact or colleague, do not resort to typing messages without vowels or shortening words for convenience. If the person suggests you text him or her, rely on proper English and avoid slang in your communication. When you do resort to "txt spk," you run the risk of being misunderstood. It's safest to use proper English, including punctuation, in all professional writing.

Don't include information in your email subject line that isn't true.
In other words, if the person did not request information, do not say so in the subject line. If you're following up after an event and you mention the name of the event, the person may be more likely to open your email.

Don't use ALL CAPS, cute icons, or emoji in your messages.
Smiley faces and "thumbs up" may be fun for text messages to friends and on Facebook, but they are usually out of place in a professional environment.

Don't go overboard with the exclamation points!!!
Even if you're excited about the topic, avoid including a lot of exclamation points in your professional communication. Some people would say to avoid them all together, but a well-placed exclamation point can convey a bit of personality—there's no need to avoid them altogether except for the most conservative professional environments, where enthusiasm of any kind may be interpreted as too casual.

Be careful your tone doesn't read negatively if that is not your intent.
It's difficult to convey the right tone in a written communication, so be aware that people may miss your intent if you're sarcastic or kidding. If the message could be interpreted as scolding in

any way, consider communicating in person so you can soften the message.

Never write anything you would not want forwarded to another person.
A colleague can easily send your message to another person, either in person or inadvertently. Think before you put anything in writing and ask yourself if there would be negative consequences if your email gained a larger audience than you intended. If so, consider conveying your message in person, instead.

Stories "outing" prominent people for being rude abound in the media. Avoid putting anything in writing that could be incriminating for you or that includes something about another person that you wouldn't want them to know you wrote. Assume everything you put in writing can become public fodder. All it takes is one person to share it via email or a social network, and the whole world (or, at least everyone at work) will be privy to your private thoughts.

Include a closing

In email, a signature may not *technically* be required. It does have your address in the "from" field, so it's not as if the reader will be confused about who sent the note. Regardless, in a professional environment, it's appropriate to include a closing. Other common ways to end your written correspondence include:

- *Thank you*
- *Best* or *Best Regards*
- *Regards*

Choose something that suits you. You may want to note what closing other people in your professional circles use and take their lead.

The only exception to these rules is if your professional contact invites you to text him or her. In that case, it is not necessary to include a formal greeting. "Dear Dr. Smith" would look out-of-place in a text, for example. However, a closing of some sort isn't a bad idea, in case your contact does not have your phone number in a list of contacts. Instead of a formal "Sincerely" or "Best," you can use a dash and your name to close a text message. For example: *-Miriam Salpeter.*

How to Handle an Introduction by Email

Everyone is busy, so written communication becomes even more important as it replaces in-person interactions more and more regularly. Email introductions are common, and you'll likely need to respond to one or more of these interactions. Keep in mind: your best bet for all professional written communication is to be clear and to the point. Remember, you're not likely to be the person you're writing's top priority, so it's up to you to make it clear what you need or how you can help. Similarly, make it easy for that person to help you.

The scenario: a mutual contact sends an email to you and another person to introduce you to each other. It's up to you to follow up and connect the dots.

Respond immediately
If you sit on the introduction and respond in a few days or a week, the person you want to meet may assume there is no urgency and may delay responding to you or avoid responding at all. If you're the one who benefits most from the introduction, and you couldn't be bothered to get in contact immediately, you've likely lost your opportunity for a timely reply from the new contact.

Immediately respond to the mutual friend directly

Thank him or her for the introduction and indicate that you'll follow up with the person immediately. Then, "Reply all" to reach the new contact, but remove the introducer's name from the "To" field. Hopefully, the initial message had a clear subject line. If it did, use it for your reply. If not, change it to something that is in line with the suggestions earlier in this chapter. For example, "Jill Jacoby said we should meet."

Indicate you are interested in building a mutually beneficial relationship

Do not focus on you and your needs. Instead, think of how you can be helpful to the person, and include that message in your response. To help clarify your message, use bold or italics to help emphasize information you want the person to notice. (Do not use all caps, however.)

Keep in mind: if your mutual introducer did not ask the new contact permission to connect you, it's possible the new networking contact is too busy or not interested in meeting or speaking with you. At this point, it's your job to inspire the person to be interested in you.

Close the loop with the introducer

When people offer to assist or go out of their way to make an introduction on your behalf, it's important to keep them in the loop regarding your progress with the person, especially if it is positive. You've presumably assured them you will follow up with their contact immediately, but be sure to also send a quick note of thanks after you meet with the contact, and especially if the interaction leads to an opportunity.

Exercise: Read the following sample email and answer the questions that follow.

Subject: *Hope we can meet soon*

Dear Betty,

I'm so glad Jill suggested we meet. She remembered we both went to the University of Tennessee and share expertise in marketing and management. As she mentioned in her introduction, I specialize in working with non-profit organizations. Since you've been executive director at ABC Non-Profit Organization for several years, she assumed we might be able to share information and resources with each other. I hope you agree.

I'd love to meet for coffee, or stop by your office on a day when you're not too busy. (I can bring some of my famous chocolate chip cookies.)

I'll look forward to hearing from you.

Best,

Margaret Allan

What key items did this sample letter include? (Select from the following):

☐ Useful heading
☐ Reference to introducer
☐ Makes a personal connection
☐ Clearly suggests a reason to meet
☐ Indicates a potential relationship builder
☐ Notes schedule issues
☐ Bolds or otherwise highlights the "ask"
☐ Provides contact information

What could this letter have done better?

_____

_____

_____

_____

Answer

The sample included these key items:

- Useful heading
- Reference to introducer
- Makes a personal connection
- Clearly suggests a reason to meet
- Indicates a potential relationship builder

Here is a list of ways this letter could have been better:

1. The subject line should have been clearer: Jill Jacoby suggested we meet.
2. Margaret could have given more information about her schedule, to make it as easy as possible for Betty to pick a date. For example:

Please let me know when might be convenient for you. I have a very flexible schedule, so I am sure I can accommodate whatever you suggest.

or

I am available every Monday, Wednesday, and Friday until 2 pm. I hope that will match your schedule.

3. The "ask" could have been in bold or underlined, as follows:

Since you've been executive director at ABC Non-Profit Organization for several years, she assumed we might be able to share information and resources with each other.

4. Finally, Margaret could have included a phone number to easily contact her.

Tips to Keep in Mind for Follow-Up Emails

There is nothing worse for your networking than attending events or meeting people, and collecting contact information and business cards, but failing to follow up with the people you met. It is up to you to follow up, and your career trajectory will improve if you follow this advice.

Keep these in mind when it comes to your follow up:

- Be timely: connect right away. The next day is not too soon.
- Include something personal, if possible. Mention a fun fact from your conversation. For example, "I hope your daughter's finals go well."
- Remind the contact of what you have to offer. This is a mutual relationship. Make a point to mention how you can help. Give without expecting anything in return.
- Don't forget to connect via LinkedIn.
- Ask for a meeting.
- Provide all the necessary information to make it as easy as possible for the person to contact and/or meet you.
- Offer your network and contacts as a resource.
- Keep in touch with your contacts, especially the people you really enjoyed meeting.

HOW TO KEEP IN TOUCH WITH YOUR FAVORITE CONTACTS

When you're meeting a lot of people, you'll encounter some you want to keep in your permanent list of contacts. Since it's never a good idea to reach out to people only when you need something from them, make a point to follow up with your best networking contacts on a regular basis. Use these apps and online tools to help you:

PhoneBook. Keep your contacts organized with notes and other useful information.

Plaxo. This cloud-based app is available on any device. It helps organize contacts into categories, such as where or how you met. It will notify you when it recognizes a contact has made a change or joined a new social network.

Newsle. Part of LinkedIn, this tool provides users updates about connections in their social networks and alerts them when one of those contacts was mentioned in the news.

Relate.ly. This app isn't free (there is a free trial), but it does everything you would ever need, including suggesting scripts for different scenarios.

Check out some of these apps and decide if they are useful for you.

How to Follow Up

If you've sent an email, included a great subject line and promises of how you can help, and posted it at a time you believe would give you the best chance of it being read, what else can you do?

48

You want to follow up without being annoying, but sometimes, it's difficult to know how to accomplish that task. Your best bet is to follow up one time in about a week if you've sent an email that requires a response. Include "Following up:_____" in the subject line of your original email.

You may want to switch gears and try to contact the person a different way. Ideally, you asked about the best way to be in touch when you initially met. Perhaps a phone call or LinkedIn message is a good secondary approach. Alternatively, you could try one of the other social media networks if the person uses them. For example, you could mention the person on Twitter if he or she uses that network. A more subtle way to get someone's attention using social media is to retweet something they posted online using their Twitter name, for example. Without even mentioning that you wish they'd reply to your message, you dropped a reminder and helped your name become more top-of-mind for the person you're trying to reach.

Exercise: Answer **True** or **False**.

_____ **1.** Subject lines are important. They should be concise and catch the reader's attention.

_____ **2.** Emails that begin with *Hey* or *Hi* are fine for colleagues if they are also friends.

_____ **3.** People who use paragraphs or bullet points to break up their email messages into more digestible bites look unprofessional and risk the contempt of others.

_____ **4.** Using humor in an email rarely works. Avoid it.

_____ **5.** Since it is important to be short and sweet when composing emails, it is perfectly okay to leave off superfluous sign offs/closings such as *sincerely* or *thank you*.

_____ **6.** When writing an email, assume it may be forwarded to others and try to imagine who else might receive it. Tailor some quick sarcastic gibes for all those who will receive your email.

_____ **7.** Thank you emails should only go out to the people who you wish to thank. Don't waste others' time with this superfluous email.

_____ **8.** Your email should mention an attachment, but shouldn't include it. If the recipient is really interested, he or she will email you reminding you to send an email with the attachment.

_____ **9.** Don't put anything in an email you wouldn't want the whole world to see.

_____ **10.** It doesn't matter what subject line you use for an introductory email.

_____ **11.** It's good to follow up with an email within two or three days.

Answers

1. **T.** Subject lines are important. They should be concise and catch the reader's attention.
2. **F.** These salutations are too informal in any work setting.
3. **F.** Using these methods make it easier for the recipient to interpret your message, which they will appreciate.
4. **T.** Using humor in an email rarely works. Avoid it.
5. **F.** These sign offs demonstrate professionalism and should be included.
6. **F.** Try to keep it simple and try to avoid negativity that might affect those who receive your forwarded email.

7. **T.** Thank you emails should only go out to the people who you wish to thank. Don't waste others' time with this superfluous email.

8. **F.** Attachments always belong with the email.

9. **T.** Emails should be professional and not a place to trash others.

10. **F.** It's usually best to use the original email from the introducer, if possible.

11. **F.** Usually, people expect you to follow up with an email in one day.

In Summary: Action Tips

- People are likely to scrutinize your written communication and judge your professionalism and abilities based on what you write. Take the opportunity to make a great first impression.

- Make the effort to select great subject lines for emails if you want people to open them. Make sure your note looks important enough to read.

- Choose your salutation and closing appropriately. Don't resort to very casual greetings, such as "Hey," or "What's new?" in your professional communication. Don't forget to add a formal ending, such as "Sincerely" to your notes and emails.

- Be aware of when you should (or should not) reply to "all."

- Read email before you respond and be careful to review before you send your messages and replies.

- Be careful what you include in emails, as they may become public when you expected them to be private.

- Be direct and prompt in your replies and format emails to be easy to read.

- Handle email introductions according to the suggestions in this chapter. Follow up and consider everyone's feelings.
- Pitch your best skills. Focus on what you can do for the person or the company. Be brief, but specific.
- Consider the day of the week and time of day when you send emails. Some research suggests Tuesdays and Saturdays are good days for email to be viewed. However, don't expect an email on Saturday to receive a reply.
- Follow up on your written email communication by using social media, to keep you top-of-mind for those who use those tools.

CHAPTER

Communicate Using Social Media: Part I

I t's important to learn how to communicate via social media, as many professional interactions occur online. When used well, social media tools provide access to new opportunities and information. Both can result in you becoming more competitive in your field. Research from the Society for Human Resource Management shows that employers are not only looking at LinkedIn—they are likely to also use Facebook and Twitter to connect with potential job applicants. Social networks make it easy for you to follow companies and brands, as well as to connect with people who might be great networking contacts.

Why Use Social Media to Network?

These networks allow you to meet people you'd never otherwise encounter from all over the world. Even if you attended every in-person networking event in your area, you could never meet the number of people you can meet networking online. Social media provides an outlet to easily share and showcase what you know with other people who may have the wherewithal to help you. You're not just networking for networking's sake. Your goal is to impress other people with your skills, experiences, and accomplishments so they will refer you for opportunities.

Learn new things

One under-considered reason for tapping into social media tools is to take advantage of the wealth of resources and streams of information and content that helps you keep your finger on the pulse of your industry. You may find yourself receiving data and information that makes you the go-to resource in your office or among your colleagues. Use this to your advantage.

Push, not pull job-search strategy

Ideally, you'd like jobs to find you instead of needing to apply for jobs. When you use social media well, you have an opportunity to magnetically attract positions to you by demonstrating expertise to people who invite you to apply for or to consider various jobs. It's the best-case scenario for anyone open to a new work experience.

Employers use it

Jobvite's research shows that 93% of employers use social networks to help make hiring decisions. They note that 73% of employers plan to increase the amount they spend pursuing employees via social networks.

Don't limit your professional social media networks to LinkedIn only. You can leverage any social network—for example, Twitter, Facebook, Pinterest, Instagram, YouTube, and others—for professional use. Your goal should be to choose the networks best suited to you and your audience and use them extensively to accomplish your networking goals.

How to Choose Networks to Use

To pick the best networks, first identify how you'd like to share your information. You have several options when it comes to sharing information online. Updates or posts will be written, spoken (as in a radio show, podcast, or video), or visual (as in video, pictures, and other images).

Think about the answers to the following questions to assess your own interests and skills.

My best skills include:

☐ Writing
☐ Speaking
☐ Taking pictures or sharing images
☐ Give me a video camera and I'll knock your socks off
☐ All of the above
☐ None of the above

When I write:

☐ I wax eloquent and enjoy long-form writing.
☐ I use as few words as possible. Who wants to read anything lengthy?
☐ Writing? Can't we just talk about it?

When I think about sharing information online, I envision it being:

☐ Words
☐ Pictures
☐ Speaking
☐ Video
☐ All of the above
☐ Do I really have to share information online?

I can easily think about sharing something on social media that is:

☐ A sentence or two
☐ At least 500 words—if not more
☐ Don't ask me to write, but I can talk up a storm
☐ I thrive on film. Lights! Camera! Action!
☐ Photography and visuals—I can share my own images!

Hopefully, this gives you a strong sense of what you enjoy and what medium works best for you. If you love the online medium you choose, you'll use it more and use it to showcase your expertise.

Look over your answers. Are you a writer, a speaker, a movie star, a photographer, or a graphic designer? Consider the following networks to correlate with each skill:

Writing skills
- *Short-form writing* (you can easily communicate something in 140 characters or less): Twitter, Facebook, LinkedIn updates
- *Long-form writing* (you enjoy writing and you're good at it): Blogging (Wordpress, LinkedIn, or another platform), Facebook, or Tumblr

Visual
- SlideShare, Pinterest, Instagram, Facebook

Speaking/video
- YouTube, Vine, BlogTalkRadio, Podcasting

Determine Your Audience

Once you know your skills and the networks that will let you take advantage of what you offer and what you enjoy, it's time to consider your audience. After all, if you love creating videos, but your intended targets don't have any time to view them, you would be wasting your efforts.

Conduct research to determine what networks most appeal to your audience. You can start by reviewing data from two key sources: Pew Internet and ComScore. These track demographics and trends related to who uses what network. However, that's just a start for those who like data. Your more important research will come from some in-depth searches to identify where your audience spends the most time.

Choose Your Networks

Once you narrow down the networks that suit your skills and see which of these overlap with your target audience, you'll know your social media sweet spot. Move forward with those networks and use them to build your professional reputation.

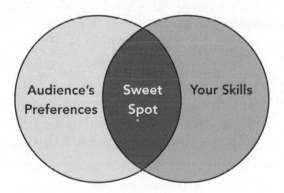

Each network has its own, unique qualities and you'll want to be sure to match your skills to what's required to be successful on each network you use. For example, if you're not capable of sending out short messages, you probably shouldn't tweet. If you are a talented writer, blog on LinkedIn's platform or start your own blog. Are you in a visual field? Did you know you can create photo collages on Twitter when you use the mobile application? Or, upload your photos on Facebook and be sure to make those posts public and searchable. If you're capable of posting great content on all of the major social media networks, by all means, do so. However, only participate where you're showing off your best professional content.

Identify your target audience and engage with them. Social networks are no longer just about connecting with friends. They offer an ecosystem of individuals, brands, and employers. Companies invest in their social media presence to give job seekers plenty of options for interesting content to like and follow.

Use these resources to get started:

LinkedIn: Groups and pulse

This is an easy choice, as professionals from every industry use LinkedIn. Determine if your audience is active in groups online. Via LinkedIn's search bar, click on the dropdown to search Groups and include keywords to find groups related to your professional interests. For example, if you're an accountant, you could search *financial experts*, *accountants*, *accounting* or *managing money*. Spend some time investigating the groups and decide if your colleagues are active enough there to warrant your time.

Pulse is LinkedIn's news and information source. It's a great way to access useful information to share on your networks (we'll explore this more later in the chapter), but it can also help you identify how involved your target audience is on LinkedIn. Follow the topics of interest and read the comments on the various posts. If there are active conversations, you'll know you've found a good resource.

Exercise: Visit LinkedIn. If you don't already have a profile, create one at LinkedIn.com. (Review my book, *Social Networking for Career Success*, for tips to prepare a terrific profile, as well as the tips later in this chapter.) Search for groups and spend time selecting topics or thought leaders in Pulse that appeal to you and would interest your target audience.

Be sure to visit the groups and review your Pulse selections frequently.

Twitter

To start, look for company names or names of people of interest via Twitter's own search toolbar.

FollowerWonk.com

This tool makes it easy to search Twitter bios. Since many people include something professional in their Twitter bios (such as keywords or company names), you can use this tool to hone in on people in your industry using Twitter.

Hashtags (#)

One of the best ways to determine if people in your field use Twitter is to search hashtags. Use the # symbol and affix it to any word related to your field. For example: #healthcare or #marketing. People use these hashtags to help attract attention for their topics from people they don't already know online, so it's a great way to find out if your potential contacts use Twitter.

Twitter Chats

Similar to hashtags, finding Twitter chats can help you hone in on the most prominent people in your professional community using the network. A Twitter chat is used when people who have similar interests hop on Twitter and tweet using a hashtag to help everyone interested get in on the conversation. There are active chats about every topic imaginable—for example, advertisers (#AdChat) or architecture (#AIAchat). You can also find chats about personal interest topics, such as a chat for foodies (#SOSfood) and one to discuss fashion and style (#styletalk). The list goes on and on. Of course, there are a lot of chats having to do with social media, and there are several other career oriented chats—#internchat and #job-huntchat, for example.

Chats give you opportunities to find people in your profession who use Twitter. Just as it is a good idea for job seekers to join a biking club if they enjoy biking, or an art class if they're artistically talented, Twitter provides an unprecedented way to reach out to new people and to extend your "loose" network—people you would otherwise never meet.

To find a link to several lists of Twitter chats, Google {Twitter chat, Keppie Careers} and you'll see an article I wrote about this topic with links to these lists.

Exercise: Visit Twitter. If you don't already have a profile, create one at Twitter.com. (Review *Social Networking for Career Success* for tips to prepare a terrific profile.)

Decide on topics that will interest you. For example, if your field is healthcare, perhaps you'll want to find people who tweet about health, or even wellness. Make a list of potential topics:

_____

_____

_____

_____

_____

Once you have your topics, visit FollowerWonk.com and search their network for the words you selected. Remember, you can include company names, too.

Go to Twitter.com and use their toolbar to search for hashtags of your topics. For example, #Healthcare or #Health. Follow and make a note of people who are using the hashtags that interest you.

As suggested, identify Twitter chats by Googling {Twitter chat, Keppie Careers}. Make a note to participate in any chats that look promising.

Facebook

Search Facebook's toolbar for groups that share your interests. Similar to groups in other networks, you may find some active, industry-related groups to access useful contacts. And, just as Twitter allows you to search hashtags online, you can also use them in Facebook, even though they are less prominent in this network.

Exercise: Follow the same advice provided about Twitter to find interesting content in Facebook. Make a note of any groups or communities that seem very useful and be sure to visit and participate often.

Instagram

You can find people you might like to follow in "Search & Explore." As Instragram's site explains, "Tap Photos to see photos and videos that people you follow have liked or that a large number of people have liked. Tap People to see accounts you might like, based on a variety of things, including who you follow, who you're connected to, and what photos and videos you like on Instagram."

Pinterest

Use the Pinterest search toolbar to conduct interest searches. Once you find people with common interests, you can see what pins they share and who follows them.

Create a Great Profile

Perhaps the most important items you write as a professional are your online bios or profiles. These have the power to connect you directly with people you need to know. Even though most of your most forward-facing bios are extremely short (such as your Linked-In headline and Twitter bio), you should put a lot of energy into ensuring they perfectly represent you and your professional brand, so you attract attention from your target audience.

How to write your LinkedIn headline

The headline appears directly under your name in LinkedIn and shows up whenever your profile comes up in search. It is your opportunity to pitch your unique value proposition—what is special about you— to anyone who comes across your profile. Does it say something that will make someone want to click through to learn more about you?

Many people include their job titles in the headline section, but that's not likely to be very compelling. Instead, include keywords that people will use when they search for someone like you as well as a promise of something you will do for them.

You have a head start on writing the perfect headline if you've already figured out how to introduce yourself in person. (See Chapter 1). Your headline will be even more succinct than the 35 or so words you chose to use when you meet people.

Use this formula:

- Identify your expertise.
- Use keywords people would naturally choose when searching for someone with your skills.
- Explain how you help.

Explain How You Help

In Chapter 1, we covered how to introduce yourself in person at a networking event. You will want to:

- Identify who you work with [*target audience*].
- Explain what you do for them [*situation/solve what problem*].
- Outline how you're effective [*results/impact*].

You'll rely on this information again for your LinkedIn headline. What is the very best thing you offer by way of professional results? If someone hires you, what can that person expect to see regarding your impact to the organization? Are you known for forming and managing well-run teams? Do you bring in top sales results? What do people say about you? Do your evaluations typically refer to a particular, marketable skill?

LinkedIn provides 120 characters for your headline—use it well. For example:

Leadership Development Management Consultant: Build effective work culture and accelerate employee performance

Researcher experienced in chemical & biological sensor / New product / Business development

Device Engineer: embedded systems architecture, analyze software & hardware; secure mobile and/or embedded devices

Monitor EEO/Affirmative Action programs, oversee training & development, create strong workplaces

Business Analyst: Develop and implement systems to bridge gaps between HR and IT organizations

Create your other social media bios

Luckily, once you've done all of that work to write your LinkedIn headline, you can simply "lather, rinse, and repeat" and use the content again for Twitter, Facebook, Pinterest, and other places with short bios. Twitter allows 160 characters, so you have a little extra space to add anything you may have left off of your LinkedIn headline.

Include the keywords that will make it easy for people who search for your expertise to find you and focus on your value proposition across social networks. Project the same message through your Twitter bio as you do on LinkedIn and other social networking profiles. Consistency is important—use every word to your advantage.

Exercise: Practice writing your LinkedIn headline (120 characters, includes all letters, spaces, and punctuation).

_____

_____

_____

_____

_____

_____

_____

_____

_____

What will you add to create a Twitter bio? (160 characters)

_____

_____

_____

_____

_____

_____

_____

_____

_____

In Summary: Action Tips

- Don't ignore opportunities to communicate via social networking tools. These networks provide terrific chances to meet new people and connect with job opportunities when necessary, since employers turn to these networks to connect with applicants.
- Social networking tools offer opportunities to learn new things and to reverse the job search process from a push (apply) to a pull (attract interest) process.
- Before you dive into social media, assess the best networks to use by determining your own skills and deciding where people you want to reach spend their time online.
- Create profiles for yourself on the networks you choose to pursue. Be sure to target your social networking bios so it's easy to find you and know about your professional specialties. Use the suggestions in this chapter to hone in on your keywords and to explain how you help.

5 Communicate Using Social Media: Part II

O ne of the most challenging aspects of communicating well on social media is learning what to say and how to say it on each of the networks. However, once you understand the types of things you should post and how to engage with new contacts, you can create a plan to identify relevant and useful information online that will interest your target audience. When you know what you're doing, it is not difficult to produce a stream of information to impress people who may refer you for opportunities—or hire you!

What to Post Online

If you're convinced using social media well can help you attract networking contacts, you're on your way to successfully using these tools to your advantage. Don't underestimate how interested hiring managers are in finding you online. Studies show many of them believe they can connect with the best candidates using social media. If you want to be considered in that group, you need to be sure to spend your time in networks where you'll be able to connect with them.

Even if you don't spend a lot of time posting content to various networks, be sure you visit, "like," or "follow" the companies that interest you—especially if you're not in a confidential job search.

Don't forget to add professional skills to your Facebook profile and make those sections public. Graph Search, Facebook's search tool, allows recruiters to search for individuals whose profile details match open jobs. You can keep friends, photos, and other aspects of your timeline private while making other profile details like job history, skills, and location visible to the public and to your next potential employer.

Here are some key tips to help you showcase your skills using social media:

Identify what's hot in your field

Before you can position yourself as an authority in your field, be sure you are up-to-date on the most recent news and information. Just as we suggested resources to help you stay on top of current events in chapter 1, you'll want to set news alerts and follow credible sources so you'll be among the first to know what people in your field need to know.

Demonstrate passion in your work

When you consistently post information relevant to your field, you make it clear how dedicated and committed you are to your work.

Help others

Forums and groups are great places to answer questions and share information with people who could use your advice. Demonstrate you're willing and able to help and you'll be a great asset for online contacts.

HOW TO FIND INFORMATION TO POST ONLINE

You may wonder where you can easily find useful information to post online. Luckily, it's very easy to find content to share. As noted in Chapter 1, the following are useful places to find information:

- **SmartBrief.com.** This service provides free newsletters covering many topics. They will send you emails that include links and summaries to articles you can easily post to your social networks with your own comments.
- **AllTop.com.** This site indexes blogs written about just about any topic. Search categories that interest you and you'll easily have your finger on the pulse of news for your industry.
- **LinkedIn Pulse.** This app in LinkedIn allows you to pull in your choice of online information sources and creates magazine-like pages with thumbnail photos and headlines from different sources.
- **Feedly.com.** This tool allows you to create a "feed" of information based on interest areas relevant for you. Once you set it up, it "feeds" you information you've selected to receive.

Make smart comments

Read everything you can find from the leaders and up-and-comers in your space, and share the best of it via social media. When you post something about what you've read, make a smart comment and mention that person's name so they know you featured their work. For example:

#2 and #5 are especially important for engagement. 10 tips to connect with your employees, by @AuthorName: [Link]

Perfect comparison of science and engineering by @AuthorName: [Link]

Interact directly with people you want to meet, especially if you've had a tough time reaching someone or attracting attention via other methods. You can use social media to indirectly access people you want to meet who also use these tools. For example, if a contact uses Twitter, find his tweets and retweet them. Include affirming messages indicating you agree with his or her information and you'll likely attract attention:

I agree with @TargetContact's assessment in this article assessing validity of solar energy: [Link]

Social media users may be easier to engage than other networking contacts. When you follow them closely, you'll likely find opportunities to respond to their questions and offer recommendations. Once you've contributed and provided value, look for signals that your target audience appreciates your insights and information. Hopefully, these people will follow you back on Twitter or other networks and respond online to your comments. Once you establish an online relationship, it's a good time to make a request for an introduction or an in-person meeting.

Become a content resource

Your goal online is to try to be indispensable. Create and curate interesting and helpful content and news. This will help you earn credibility and learn a lot, and will enable you to be better prepared for interviews and your next job. For example:

Latest update from the NDFB about ABC [Link]

Post and share useful information online via LinkedIn, Facebook, and Twitter. If you're a good writer, you can also consider creating a blog, or offer to contribute content to other established blogs your new contacts manage. When you follow this advice, you can warm up cold calls and open doors that may have otherwise stayed closed.

What Employers Like to See Online

Assume employers will review anything you post online, so provide a stream of content and information they can only view as positive. Recruiters like to see responsible photos and content from people who take their personal brand image and work seriously. They are most likely to judge you first based on your LinkedIn profile, but will likely tap into any other online content they can access.

EXPERT INSIGHT: WHAT ONE RECRUITER LOOKS FOR ONLINE

I interviewed Jackie Hydock, Director, Global Recruiting at App Annie. She explained what they seek in new employees:

"What we are looking for is good judgment. As we recruit, we keep in mind that every App Annie employee is also an App Annie brand ambassador, and we want to make sure our team is made up of those who will reflect our company in the most positive light everywhere—whether they're on the conference show floor or in the gym."

The organization taps social media tools to recruit, and she made the following suggestions regarding how job seekers can use social media effectively:

"Candidates should post content directly to career sites or mention employers. We love gaining new candidate followers and appreciate it when followers like, comment, retweet, or favorite our #lifeatappannie and App Annie Instagram posts. A couple of candidates have tweeted that they sent in their applications to App Annie and couldn't wait to hear from us! It's also exciting when followers retweet or favorite specific job openings. Engaging with us through our social media channels is a great way to stand out among the applicant pool. It shows us that candidates

continued from page 71

have taken the time to learn more about our company's culture, values, and beliefs, which is an integral part of our recruiting process. If a candidate is already a user of our App Annie products and broadcasts that on social media—that's another major plus in our eyes."

She also said, "Any attention a candidate gives to our corporate or recruiting social sites makes us feel like they are eager to stay connected and that they want to engage with us. We appreciate the candidates who take time to follow us, whether they are interested in working with us today or just hoping to keep us in mind for the future. If a candidate goes the extra mile to share a job opening with his or her network, it is a great sign that he or she would be a positive addition to our growing team. It is our commitment to our followers to keep our feeds interesting and filled with fun and unique App Annie content."

Use Social Media to Illustrate Your Professionalism

Soft skills, or emotional intelligence, are very valuable to hiring managers. Research suggests managers are beginning to put more weight on abilities that are difficult to teach, such as leadership, communication, and adaptability. When you use social media to communicate information and insights, you can easily demonstrate many of the most valued soft skills. For example, if your target job requires good judgment and a positive demeanor, your active Twitter stream, devoid of negative comments and without any questionable content, becomes a living example of how you may perform on the job.

Additionally, social media provides an opportunity to consistently demonstrate your ability to communicate concisely and completely, even in only 140 characters, which is the length of the longest tweet. Do not underestimate the value of being able to prove what you state on your resume or application materials via your social networks.

For example, if leadership is a skill you'd like to demonstrate, consider finding a Twitter chat to join. These chats, which exist in just about any field you can imagine, are great ways to improve your standing in your online community. Once you become active in a chat, you can offer to help the chat leaders administer the chat by guest hosting. Ultimately, you may find starting your own chat is a useful way to highlight your leadership abilities.

Privacy and professionalism (everyone sees everything)

If you haven't Googled your name recently, it's time to do a quick search to identify what comes up. If you're unhappy with the results, you should take the time to clean up your content. Do not assume because your settings are "private" on Facebook, for example, your content is secure. If you research the topic, there are many stories of people who believed they were sharing information only with their close friends online, only to later find out someone reposted or shared their information with someone else.

Even if you aren't connected with your colleagues or boss in your social networks, avoid posting or writing anything negative about work. Do not mention customers with less than positive comments and do not share anything on social media that would concern your boss, co-workers, or people you hope will hire you.

What not to post online

It would be impossible to list everything you should not write on social media. Jobvite's Annual Social Recruiting survey of employers who use social media to hire people, detailed a list of particularly egregious items to keep off of your social media feeds.

Their research suggested employers found the following items most damaging on a candidate's digital profile. The number illustrates the percent of respondents who viewed it negatively:

- Illegal drug references 83%
- Sexual posts 70%
- Spelling/grammar mistakes 66%
- Profanity 63%
- Guns 51%
- Alcohol 44%

Interestingly, respondents indicated they view political comments and commentary as mostly "neutral" (69%). However, it's still a good idea to avoid getting caught up in highly charged political discussions online. Also, be aware that even if you're joking about illegal drugs or other similar topics—employers are not amused. Avoid posting any information that a reader could construe negatively.

VOLUNTEERING? TELL THE WHOLE WORLD

In the Jobvite survey, 65% of respondents viewed volunteering and donating to charity favorably. So, if you regularly volunteer or are involved in a charitable cause, make a point to post it to your social media networks. In LinkedIn, you can even feature it as part of your profile.

A good rule is to avoid sharing anything online that you wouldn't want posted on a public billboard, such as photos of you acting or dressing unprofessionally. You'll also want to avoid off-color or prejudicial jokes or comments. In general, it's a good idea to avoid excessive or frequent complaints online, even if you're just talking about yourself. You don't want someone who sees your profile to think you are always sick or constantly angry.

Bottom line: assume everything you post is public. Don't write anything about anyone you wouldn't say to him or her in person and don't share something if you don't want people to associate that information with you and judge your qualifications as a result.

In Summary: Action Tips

- Visit, like, or follow the companies that interest you—especially if you're not in a confidential job search—and decide on a plan for what you can share online to demonstrate your expertise.
- Use the resources listed in this chapter as a guide to find useful content you can share and cultivate your own list of content resources.
- Reach out to networking contacts by mentioning their names via social networks and attract attention by becoming a source of information for your colleagues.
- Keep in mind, if you're a job seeker, that employers appreciate seeing information about your volunteer work and frown on bad grammar and mentions of illegal drug use. Be aware that everything you post is public. Make sure your social media streams work in your favor and not against you.

II JOB SEARCH MATERIALS

6 Communicate Your Value Proposition in Your Resume

Some people tout the "death" of the resume, because they believe online profiles will replace this traditional job search tool. Online profiles are important. However, for most people, the resume is still a crucial marketing document. How can you communicate what you offer employers via your resume so they want to hire you?

Understand Your Resume's Purpose

It's natural to think your resume is all about you. After all, it has your name at the top, and everything on it refers to you. Ironically, the content should actually focus as much on your desired employer as it does on your own background. Employers are interested in what you have to offer them as it relates to the job description. Your job is to draw a clear connection between your skills and accomplishments and what the employer wants. Keep in mind: most

COMMUNICATE YOUR VALUE PROPOSITION IN YOUR RESUME

companies evaluate resumes via an Applicant Tracking System (ATS)—a computer that scans for key words—or a busy recruiter or hiring manager visually scans them for 10–20 seconds each. Get to the point and make it clear why you are perfect for the job, or you won't have much of a chance of landing an interview.

SHOULD YOU BRAG IN YOUR RESUME?

It is okay to brag a little bit in your resume. However, be sure to provide specifics to back up every item. Also, keep in mind, employers frown on the "perfectionists" with strong "attention to detail" who have typos or grammatical errors in their job search documents!

Target Your Resume

It's not difficult to target a resume. Find keywords in the job description and in the organization's website. Focus on job requirements and evaluate how you have what it takes to solve the employer's problems. Incorporate skills, accomplishments, and results in your resume; don't just write a laundry list of "stuff" you've done. Always consider the employer's perspective. Will he or she know why you are a good fit based on your resume? If not, revise your materials to make a clear connection.

Exercise: Choose several job descriptions that interest you. Copy and paste the information into a file and highlight all of the parts of the descriptions that apply to you. Ideally, you will highlight all (or most) parts of the materials. Review the highlighted details and underline all of the words that seem to come up more than once. Those are most likely to be the keywords you should include in your resume.

Make a list here of the most important keywords:

_____

_____

_____

_____

_____

_____

_____

Appeal to Employers

Each word on your resume should be designed to attract your target audience. Keep the following tips in mind when writing your resume to ensure your focus is on the employers.

Incorporate accomplishments and skills

Resumes written to feature a laundry list of "stuff" usually fail to land interviews. What you've done in your past may be relevant, but don't forget to incorporate language addressing your skills and accomplishments. If you worked on a team, indicate your specific role in the end product. For example:

Used written and oral communication skills as team lead in charge of creating presentation to executive board. CEO commented on accurate and detailed results.

Include links in your online contact information

Include links to social media profiles (such as your LinkedIn URL) in your resume's contact information. If you use other social media tools professionally (such as Twitter, Facebook, Instagram, or other networks), include that information as well. Providing links will help employers who evaluate your resume get a better picture of you as a candidate who is keeping up with modern communication tools. Use a professional email that doesn't reference your age or family status. (For example, avoid "pop@hotmail.com," "Brices-Mom@gmail.com," or JudySmith1989@yahoo.com.)

Consider the aesthetics of your resume

Your resume doesn't need to be in Arial or Times New Roman font. To create a more modern look, consider expanding your font choices to include: Georgia, Calibri, Tahoma, or Geneva. Don't use more than one font in your resume unless you're a graphic designer, and don't overdo it with the underlines and bolds. Be consistent. For example, if you bold one job title, be sure to bold all of them.

Use headlines to feature your expertise

Keep in-step with today's trends by creating headlines for your resume instead of an objective. For example, take a look at the "before" and "after" highlights for a candidate looking for a medical administrative assistant job:

Before—Objective
Innovative, highly motivated, dynamic team player with extensive experience, stellar writing skills, and the ability to effectively manage concurrent projects seeks opportunity to contribute in hospital setting.

After—Headline

Medical Administrative Assistant / Unit Secretary / Clerical Expert
Maintain Confidentiality—Coordinate With All Stakeholders
Strong Oral and Written Communication Skills / Organized /
Reliable / Quick Thinking

The "after" example includes job titles and specifics directly from the job description that describe relevant, necessary skills.

Exercise: What are some problems with the following resume header? List everything you would improve.

Jill Jack

555 Angel Way – Chicago, IL – 312-555-0000 – Jill.Jack@hotmail.com

Objective

Innovative, highly motivated, dynamic team player with extensive experience, stellar writing skills, and the ability to effectively manage concurrent projects seeks opportunity to contribute in Fortune 500 company.

_____

_____

_____

_____

_____

_____

Answer

- It does not include social media references, and relies on an old-fashioned email address. (While I, personally, don't discriminate against an "AOL," or "Hotmail" address, it can make you appear a little dated and not in tune with modern technology.) Consider a Gmail account, with the added benefit of a Google profile.
- Your objective is to get the job. There is no need for a formal "Objective." Use that space to include headlines and bullet points describing your fit for the job. In addition, the objective here uses overused words (innovative, highly motivated, dynamic, extensive experience). These words are not very descriptive; avoid "empty" words in your resume.
- It doesn't have a clear focus or specific job goal.

Here is the header rewritten into a stronger format:

Jill Jack

123 Main St. – New York, NY – 212.555.0000 – JillJack@gmail.com
http://www.linkedin.com/in/JillJack – @JillJack – JillJack.com
Multimedia Manager – Communications Strategist –
Content Developer

Market savvy, writer/editor experienced in producing profitable online, video, and eZine content.

"Jill combines a flair for the creative and an intuitive understanding of market trends and consumer needs with her unbeatable technical, writing, editing, and management skills. I've never known anyone who can evaluate the landscape, design a strategy, and execute on plans as well as Jill."

—Peter Pan, Overseeing Editor, XYX Company
(View this and other endorsements via LinkedIn.)

What's better about this header?

It incorporates social media URLs—indicating this person is involved online and up-to-date. By inviting the reader to review her Twitter stream and LinkedIn profile for additional information, it's clear (no matter how old this job seeker may be) the candidate is tech-savvy and clearly to learn new things. Only showcase these URLs if you are using social media professionally. However, assume people will find your Twitter and other social media outlets.

Notice this resume includes a link to the job seeker's personal website (otherwise known as a social resume). Having this online portfolio really demonstrates she is using technology and is up-to-date. This header uses important resume real estate at the top of the document to hone in on important points: job titles and key skills. It avoids "empty" words that don't describe a connection between the candidate and the job. It's important to select key words from job descriptions, company websites, and LinkedIn profiles from others in your industry. It also includes a recommendation from someone found on LinkedIn. This is a great way to help tell your story and to prove your qualifications from an outside perspective.

Now, write your resume headline:

_____

_____

_____

_____

_____

_____

_____

_____

_____

_____

Avoid empty words

Notice the "before" objective includes *highly motivated*, *dynamic*, and *team player*. None of these words help the reader learn something specific about the candidate. Do not waste space with generalities. The more targeted you can be, the more vibrant and interesting your resume appears.

Avoid functional resume formats

Functional resumes focus on the job seeker's skills without emphasizing when and where he or she used those skills. This sounds tempting if you are trying to camouflage your age. The problem is, hiring managers like to know when and where you used the skills you say you have. Many will assume someone using this format is trying to hide something. Since you don't want to arouse suspicion, stick to a reverse chronological format, where you describe your most recent experience first, and include dates.

WHAT ABOUT GRADUATION DATES?

You may choose to leave off the year you earned your degree(s), but assume that if you do, the person reading your resume may think you are older than you are.

Don't include every job you've ever had

No one is interested in your autobiography. Employers mainly need to know about your most recent experience as it relates to what they want you to do for them. If you were a banker 20 years ago, but are now applying for marketing positions more in line with your recent experience, there's no need to focus on ancient history. It's perfectly acceptable to only include the last 10 years of your professional experience. You may even choose to headline the section, "Recent Experience." If it is relevant, summarize work you did more than 10 years ago at the end without describing it in detail.

Avoid jargon

You may have seen articles disparaging use of jargon or buzzwords in resumes and LinkedIn profiles. Be careful if you purge your materials of the language employers are expecting in your resume. The best approach is to mirror the job description. If it is full of jargon, be sure you include at least some of those keywords in your materials. However, be sure you don't just stuff your document with empty language. Make it clear how those industry buzzwords relate to your experience and accomplishments. Be specific and employers won't view your resume as being full of empty language.

Don't mention "references available on request"

When you include this comment, readers will assume you are out of touch with modern resume expectations. The reader knows you will provide references; it does not need to appear on your materials.

Connect to Your Target Employer

When you write your resume, identify what the employer needs and make a clear case for why you are a good fit. In other words, think first about what your audience (the employer) would want to know, and include that information in your resume. Eliminate details not relevant to the job.

Resume "Don't" Checklist

Check your resume for these overly self-centered red flags.

An objective

Does your resume include a line or two at the top that says: "Seeking a position with a growing company where I will feel fulfilled and get experience necessary to achieve my goals"? While most objectives are not quite so self-centered, the nature of the objective is that it focuses on the job seeker and not the employer. In other words, it's all about you and what you want. The employer does not care about your needs, so any language focused on you is a waste of space on your resume. In addition, the objective is a dated vestige of resume days gone by; avoid it in favor of a headline and quick bullet points to clearly connect with the employer's needs.

I, me, or my

While some resumes do include first-person language, in general, resumes should be written in the first person implied voice. For example, "Managed 20 employees" instead of "I managed 20 employees." If your resume is peppered throughout with self-referential language, it will probably strike the reader as a bit "me centric."

Oversharing

It's very nice that your family is the most important aspect of your life, but the resume isn't the place to discuss it. Refrain from including too much personal information that does not relate to the job's requirements. When you do spend too much space talking about yourself, it indicates you are preoccupied with what you want or need instead of what the employer wants from you. In the United States, resumes should never include personal information, such as age, marital status, or religious affiliation.

Beware of seeking experience

If you were hiring, would you want to choose someone who hopes to gain experience by doing the job or would you more likely select a candidate who already has the needed skills? It's rare for an employer to want to hire someone who does not already have the background and skills necessary to do the job. If you are looking for experience, that is fine, but keep it to yourself and focus on the skills you do have to help qualify you for the job.

Unnecessary details

No, you don't need to list every job you've ever held for the past 25 years on your resume. Generally, it's appropriate to include the last 10 or 15 years of experience, but be sure to focus on the most relevant experience. Especially if you're transitioning to a new field, feature the experience in past jobs that's more relevant and interesting to your new target employer. Don't spend a lot of time listing things you've done that have nothing to do with your goals.

How many of these "don't do this" items are on your resume? How do you plan to change these to ensure that you have a more modern, useful marketing document?

_____

_____

_____

_____

_____

_____

REPRESENT YOUR CAREER STAGE

Be sure your resume represents your career stage. For example, if this is not your first job out of school, you may want to consider moving your "education" section from the top of your document to the end.

Avoid careless errors

Errors, even small typos or missing commas, can be devastating on a resume. Some employers will not pursue a candidate with errors on a resume because they believe mistakes suggest the candidate is not attentive to details. Since being detail-oriented is a key requirement for so many jobs, that's a real concern. It's a challenge to notice mistakes when you edit your own work. Follow these suggestions to help ensure your resume is error free.

- Highlight sections in bright colors before you read them.
- Increase the font size so it's easier to see each character.
- Read sentences backward and forward.
- Read the document's pages in reverse order.
- Print a hard copy and use a tube highlighter to mark the mistakes.
- Read sentences aloud.
- Create an exclusion dictionary in Word. (Google it to learn how.)
- Use online tools such as Grammarly.com.
- Ask a friend with good proofreading skills to help with your resume or hire a proofreader.
- Put down your resume for a day and re-proofread it with fresh eyes after you've had a break.

It is well worth your time to take the extra steps to double check your work when putting the finishing touches on your resume. If you can avoid even one mistake, it might make the difference between a chance at an interview and being tagged as a careless applicant.

Never lie

"Seeking liars; apply within." It's an unlikely headline for any job description. While some employers may be lazy and fail to confirm credentials before hiring certain applicants, people who embellish their qualifications or lie about them are always at risk for losing their positions—even after having worked in the job for years. You only need to Google {lies on resumes} to find stories of people in impressive positions who lost their jobs because they falsified their resumes years ago. Your goal should be to present the best possible impression consistent with the truth.

If you don't want to be looking over your shoulder or hoping no one in HR gets suspicious and decides to audit their files, avoid these whoppers on your resume:

- Lies about past employers. Do not lie about where you worked, even if you think it sounds impressive to pad your resume with big-name employers. It's very easy to verify employment, even via a quick review of LinkedIn contacts and an email or two.
- Lies of omission. If you think failing to mention key points will keep you out of trouble, think again. "You never actually asked me if I graduated with a degree" will not serve as a good excuse if you're approached about lying about your academic credentials, which may be listed in an ambiguous manner on your resume. Leaving dates off your resume and failing to disclose other details is not wise.
- Half-truths. Plan to leave a job off your resume because you were only there for a short time? Keep in mind, there is a lot of scrutiny on new hires, and if a company conducts a background check, you'll need to be prepared to explain why you didn't want anyone to know you worked at a company. You don't want to raise any red flags or spook employers who might wonder what else they don't know about you before they hire you.

- Little embellishments. You may have read about how personal branding is an important part of marketing yourself for a job, but you may have incorrectly assumed boosting your qualifications was part of growing your brand. Avoid embellishing your titles, your mentors, or your skills and accomplishments on your resume and you're much more likely to land a job that's the right fit for you. Avoid this big job search mistake if you want to find—and keep—your next job.

Review Your Resume

Evaluate your resume based on these crucial items and you will be well prepared to engage with your targeted employers. Ask yourself the following questions.

Does my resume target my audience?

Every job and each employer seeks a slightly different applicant. Unless you are applying for the same exact job over and over again, you should not be sending the identical resume for every position. Research your target organizations. Use their buzzwords and lingo in your application materials. (You can easily tweak a well-written resume to appeal to different audiences, so don't feel that you need to completely rewrite your resume for each new job.)

Does my resume require the reader to fill in the blanks?

This unconscious assumption that you can allude to a skill or accomplishment on your resume and the employer will make the connection that you're great for the job is one of the biggest job seeker mistakes. Do not assume someone will stop to analyze what you mean when you use vague language or indicate that you "assisted with" a project, for example. If you are not clear about what you offer and how it relates to the job, the only thing you should assume is that you won't get the interview.

Is my resume attractive, consistent, error-free, and easy to read?

Don't underestimate how important it is to have a clear, error-free, visually impressive resume. Does your resume look crowded with thick text blocks that may be difficult to scan? Are you making strong use of bold to enhance your document, or are you overdoing it? Did you use a resume template from your word processing software? (Don't!) Since readers likely give your resume a 20-second glance, visual appeal is important. If the reader notices careless spelling errors, it is not likely that you will land an interview.

Do you DEMONSTRATE what you have to offer?

Is your resume a laundry list of jobs you've held, or does it engage the reader and demonstrate your skills and achievements? You should quantify your value using percentages, numbers, and specifics. Your resume should highlight the positive impact that you had in previous jobs. You want to convince readers that you could do the same for them. Make sure your resume is targeted, attractive, and demonstrates what you have to offer and you'll be on your way to an interview soon.

In Summary: Action Tips

- Be sure you understand the resume's purpose. It's a marketing document to help an employer understand what you offer. It's not intended to be all about you. Avoid including too much information that doesn't apply directly to the employer.
- Target the resume by choosing keywords that make it easy for someone to see why you're a good fit for the position.
- Incorporate accomplishments and skills. Avoid creating a resume that's nothing more than a list of "stuff" you've done. Include results of your work and detail how the organization benefitted from your skills.
- Don't forget to include social media links on your resume and create and use an email that doesn't showcase your age or family status.
- Pay attention to how your resume looks. Choose modern-looking fonts and don't overdo bolds, italics, and underlines.
- Do not use an objective section; instead, use headlines to feature your expertise and make sure your resume isn't overly self-centered.
- Avoid careless errors at all costs. Edit your resume and ask a competent friend to look it over, too. Use the tips in this chapter to help you edit your own work if necessary.
- Never lie on a resume. You will be sorry later.

7

Write a Cover Letter that Knocks Their Socks Off

Once you create a resume that demonstrates your strengths and clearly connects your abilities to the employer's needs, it's time to author a cover letter to support your candidacy. Similar to your resume, which is a marketing document, a cover letter is a sales pitch. The best cover letters provide enticing introductions to your resume and are interesting enough to inspire readers to want to read more about you.

How can you achieve that goal? Similar to the resume, when you write your cover letters, put yourself in the employer's shoes. What are they most likely interested in learning about you? How can you create a note that leaves them wanting to know more about you?

What to Include in Your Cover Letter

1. **Explain exactly why you're interested in the job.** Most people send the same cover letter to every job. If you want

to stand out from the crowd, include specific details and information that explain why you are a perfect fit for this particular opportunity.

2. **Feature your skills and accomplishments to convince an employer that you'll be an asset from day one.** Don't just say you're great for the job. Prove it by providing several details to help convince the reader they can't live without you.

3. **Include some personal information, or a story.** A story will help connect you compellingly to the opportunity.

4. **Don't forget to let them know what you want: an interview.** A call-to-action is a must on a cover letter.

Once you create a template for your cover letter, you will be able to reuse it and produce customized letters for different employers. Spend extra time to create one great organized letter and you'll be on your way to easy cover letter writing down the road.

Salutation

Always address your letter to a specific person's name. Never address a cover letter generically. Make a valiant effort to identify a name. If you can't find the information online, contact the company to ask for the correct name and use your Internet research skills to see if you can confirm a specific person to send your letter. As a very last resort, "Dear Hiring Manager" will work in a pinch, especially if the company has gone to great lengths to shield the exact name from the applicant pool. Do not resort to sexist salutations, such as "Dear Sir."

Opening Pitch

This is where you sell yourself. Why are you right for the job? Select your cues from the job description, which is usually very detailed and lengthy. Evaluate what is most important to the employer and emphasize those details in your letter.

Take advantage of all the information available to you in the job description to craft a spot-on first sentence that will appeal to your readers. Your first paragraph should focus on what you have to offer relative to the employer's needs. In the past, coaches encouraged job seekers to start their letters, "I saw your ad in X publication and am writing to apply for the position of _____." You do need to state the position in which you have an interest, but this should not lead your letter. Of course you are applying for the job—so is everyone else! What makes you special or unique? That is how to lead your letter.

Be interesting

If you send a formulaic letter with nothing more interesting than the fact that you are applying for job number 123 and that you saw the ad in XYZ.com, you won't pass the cover letter test for sticklers who use the cover letter as a benchmark to choose great candidates. Make sure you write an interesting letter. Don't miss the opportunity to make a great connection between what the employer wants and what you have to offer.

Not everyone has a great story or a reason for applying for a position. If you do, the cover letter is the place to tell it. For example, if you are a runner, applying to a company that makes your favorite running shoes, include it in your cover letter. Was this the company where you launched your career, and you are ready to come back? Say so. Did you always admire the organization's television ads growing up, and now you are applying to help create new ones while working for them? That's another great story for your cover letter.

AVOID BORING BEGINNINGS

Do not start your letter with, "Hello, my name is Janet Miles." Your name goes at the end of your letter, and it's also on the resume, so it sounds juvenile and boring to include it in the lead to your cover letter.

Which is a more interesting introduction to a cover letter?

A:

To Whom It May Concern:

I am writing to apply for the accountant job advertised on Career-Builder. I have a lot of experience with accounting and I'm excited about the opportunities your organization offers. It seems like working for a company that builds playground equipment would be a lot of fun.

B:

Dear Jack Spratt:

As an accountant with a passion for playgrounds, I couldn't believe my eyes when I saw the advertisement for the accounting position you posted on CareerBuilder. For the past five years, I've led a team of volunteers in my town to reimagine and rebuild our playgrounds. As it happens, I am tasked with researching the best, environmentally and child-friendly materials, and I always choose your equipment!

Hopefully, you can see that B makes for a much more compelling opener—one that will make the hiring manager want to read more.

Exercise: Use this space to write down a few story-oriented items you could use to relate to some of the jobs that appeal to you:

_____

_____

_____

_____

_____

_____

Identify Your Skills

Even if you have a great story or connection to the organization, you must emphasize the skills you have for the job. If you've already written your resume, it should be pretty easy to identify your best skills. Don't forget to use the job description as your guide. Just as you targeted the employer when writing your resume, do the same with your cover letter. Include specifics to appeal to the employer.

Exercise: List the most important skills for the jobs that interest you. If you can't remember, review the keywords you chose for your resume in Chapter 6. List the items in order (most important first) from the job description.

_____

_____

_____

For each important item, write one sentence to illustrate how you have that skill. Include a skill related to the item. For example:

From job description: Assemble highly confidential and sensitive information
Your notes: _As assistant to the executive vice president, I frequently collected and evaluated confidential and sensitive information. I demonstrate analytical abilities and strong judgment when determining how to handle these documents._

From job description: Handle diverse group of callers and visitors
Your notes: _Display excellent in-person and telephone communication skills when directing diverse groups of potential clients._

From job description: Plan, prioritize, and organize supervisor's schedule
Your notes: _Easily manage and organize multiple priorities so my supervisor's schedule is uncomplicated and easy to follow._

Use your list to populate your cover letter with relevant details to illustrate your qualifications for your "opening pitch."

A sample opening line to accompany these items might be:

As a detail oriented executive assistant skilled in managing multiple priorities, including confidential information and directing a diverse group of clients, I support my supervisor and ensure she is prepared for any eventuality.

_____

_____

_____

_____

_____

_____

_____

_____

Highlight Your Qualifications

The second part of your letter should feature the qualifications that make you perfect for the job. Don't hesitate to research the organization beyond the job description to find links between their needs and your skills. For example, if they feature their values prominently in the job description, incorporate some of those relevant details into your letter.

Use bullet points to group your qualifications. Choose three headers and select no more than three bullet points for each header. You can use parts of your resume to populate your cover letter, but do not simply repeat your resume. You want to use the letter as a hook to make the reader want to learn more by reviewing your resume.

For example, assume you are applying for an editorial assistant job and you identify the key aspects of the job to include the following:

- Provide clerical and logistical support to editor
- Serve as liaison with authors and the community
- Maintain a database

Create headlines using those items and list two or three bullet points under each headline to indicate your skills in those areas. An example for the first headline might be:

Clerical and Logistical Skills
- Efficiently process and sort incoming mail and answer and direct all phone calls for supervisor, allowing her to attend to a busy schedule.
- Manage and handle correspondence, files, and submissions for busy editorial office. Known for ability to quickly reply to inquiries, eliminating need for follow-up.
- Accurately file inquiries and requests, allowing supervisor to easily find needed materials on a moment's notice.

Call to Action

Don't leave your reader hanging. Be clear regarding what you want to accomplish: getting an interview. Include a call-to-action at the end of your cover letter. In your closing, ask for an opportunity to interview for the position and indicate when you will follow up if you do not hear back from them. However, don't go overboard. Unless you are applying for a sales job, think twice before including language such as, "I'll call you on Friday to schedule an interview." This may be a turnoff for some hiring managers. It's best to indicate you hope they agree you're a good match and you will follow up as of a certain date. You could alienate the employer if you act as if you are in charge of the process.

Sample Cover Letter

Here's a sample cover letter for a job as an administrative assistant for a healthy food company (SnackBetter) that puts all of the elements together:

Dear Ms. Munch:

My friends call me "Ms. Healthy" because I am always suggesting they trade out their unhealthy chips and candy for something more nutritious. What do I always offer in exchange? SnackBetter treats! Imagine my excitement when I saw the administrative assistant opening at your company (#1510) on CareerBuilder this morning. I am a big fan of your company, and especially appreciate the company's commitment to serving the community and protecting the environment. However, those are just a few reasons why I am a perfect fit for the position.

Highlights of Qualifications

Clerical and Logistical Skills
- *Efficiently process and sort incoming mail and answer and direct all phone calls for supervisor, allowing her to manage a busy schedule.*

- *Oversee and handle correspondence, files and submissions for busy editorial office. Known for ability to reply quickly to requests, eliminating need for follow-up.*

- *Accurately file inquiries and requests, allowing supervisor to easily find needed materials on a moment's notice.*

Excellent Verbal and Written Communication Abilities
- *Warmly greet visitors, ensure they have everything they need and direct them to appropriate waiting areas, resulting in visitors leaving office with positive feelings about the organization and brand.*

- *Frequently called on to create correspondence templates for executives to ensure all necessary information is efficiently communicated.*

- *Manage multiple phone lines and direct all inquiries to the right resources.*

Technologically Savvy

- *Easily work with multiple office software programs, including spreadsheets, databases, and word processing and graphic presentation software.*

- *A quick study, learned new research application program so well, my supervisor asked me to create a training program for other staff members.*

- *Use multiple social media platforms to help enhance employer's brand, including LinkedIn, Twitter, Facebook, Instagram, and Pinterest.*

Based on how well the job description overlaps with my background and accomplishments, I believe I would be able to easily contribute on day one at your organization. I hope you agree, and invite you to review my resume (attached). Please contact me via email or phone (212-555-5555) to schedule a time for us to speak. I will follow up with you the week of June 15 if I do not hear from you before that time. I look forward to working for an organization whose products I use and enjoy and whose values are so closely aligned with mine.

Sincerely,

Eata Healthy

Video Cover Letters

In today's hyper-connected world, don't be surprised if you have an opportunity to include a video cover letter for a job. Many employers who are seeking an efficient and effective way to evaluate applicants are investigating ways to incorporate video technology into their hiring practices. Susan Vitale, chief marketing officer at iCIMS, a provider of innovative Software-as-a-Service talent acquisition solutions, says 65 percent of employers are adding video technology to learn about job seekers' personalities and professionalism before scheduling on-site or phone interviews.

If your target employer prompts you to include a video aspect to your application, consider the following tips from Vitale to create a job-winning video cover letter.

Do your research
As a job seeker, it's up to you to assess your audience and target all of your materials to appeal to the employer. Hone in on the company's value proposition (what it offers) and its mission statement. Don't forget to review the company's press kits if they're shared online; they can provide a lot of insightful information. Read everything you can about the organization and the people in the department where you'd like to work. Tap LinkedIn, Facebook, and Twitter to access information other candidates may not bother to find.

Expand your channels
If you really want to be creative and targeted, include on-screen text and other types of visual imagery that add more depth and meaning to your video. When you incorporate multimedia in your video, you demonstrate your tech-savvy skills.

Learn from others
Use YouTube as a reference tool. Search for video cover letters and see how others put together their materials.

Practice makes perfect

Don't plan to create your video in one sitting. You want to be sure to appear confident, natural, and relaxed, and that takes practice. Write a short script and be sure to reference the items in the job description that make you stand out.

Be concise

"Short and sweet" should be your mantra. Most people have limited attention spans and hiring executives who are in active need of new hires are extremely busy. You can actually say a lot in 30 seconds. Try to keep your video succinct.

Cover Letter Don'ts Checklist

Do not:

- Forget to include a cover letter. If they ask for it, it's part of following instructions.
- Assume everyone will read it. Keep in mind, while it is important to write a strong cover letter, never include crucial information in the cover letter that you don't cover in your resume.
- Add your cover letter as a separate attachment with a short introduction. Incorporate the body of the cover letter in your email if you are emailing it to the employer.
- Bore the reader with a trite, recycled letter suitable for every job that interests you.
- Rehash your resume. Be sure to include something extra and interesting in your cover letter beyond what is in your resume.
- Forget to include a great story that ties you to the position.
- Write a cover letter that is all about you, your wants, and your needs. Use the opportunity to connect with the reader based on what he or she wants to know. Review the checklist

in Chapter 6 to help identify red flags that your resume is all about you, and apply them to the cover letter, too.

- Include typos or errors. These are the kiss of death. Even if the job does not require you to wax eloquent regularly or to create written materials for the company, if you misspell words or send a letter with typos and grammatical errors, it's a mark against you in a competitive field. Edit your own note carefully and ask a trusted friend to review it. Read it out loud to be sure you haven't left off words or made a typo that spell-check doesn't pick up—for example, if you've said, "I'd be a terrific manger" instead of "manager," spell check will not alert you to the mistake.

- Accidentally misaddress your letter to another company with a similar job opening. Double check the employer and be sure to address it properly.

- Exaggerate or lie. Don't say you are perfect for the job if you are not.

- Be too humble. If you really ARE perfect for the job, make a case for yourself. The opposite of the braggart, who is "ideal" for every job, the overly humble job seeker may actually apologize for applying and explain the skills he or she does not have for the job. The "why I'm not qualified" strategy is less than optimal! You may apply for jobs that are a reach. When you do, focus on what makes you a good fit and don't dwell on the negatives.

- Include unflattering details about your past jobs or reasons why you may not be a perfect fit. The cover letter isn't the place for full disclosure. Don't include any information about what you cannot do or what skills you do not have. Focus on the positive.

- Focus on training. You may think your most important qualification is your MBA or your recent bachelor's degree. Even if the degree or training is a requirement, everyone who applies will have that qualification. Focus on what makes you capable of helping the organization beyond your degrees.

- Leave things in the employer's court. Instead, say something such as, "I'll follow up with you on _____" and hope to have the opportunity to discuss how my qualifications are a good fit for your needs."

That's a lot of "don'ts" for one piece of your job search correspondence. Don't be discouraged by this long list. Keep in mind, when you write an accurate, targeted, typo-free cover letter addressed to the right person and reference the correct job, you'll be ahead of most other candidates. While you should not write a novel, if you can say something personal to connect your skills and background to the job (referencing the job description), that will make your letter stand out even more. For example, you may include a relevant anecdote. If you're applying to work at a company that makes running shoes, and your first pair of special shoes came from them, mention it. Keep it targeted and make a one-to-one connection that indicates why you are a good fit based on the job description, and you will be in very good shape.

In Summary: Action Tips

- The cover letter is a tricky piece of correspondence, because it is both very important and may be ignored. Regardless, you enhance your chances of landing an interview when you write a great cover letter that ties directly to the employer's needs.

- Include details about why (exactly) you're interested in the job. Don't send a generic cover letter. Explain why you are perfect by adding a story or relevant personal information, if possible.

- Always address your letter to a specific person's name. If that's impossible, choose something non-sexist, such as "Dear Hiring Manager." Never resort to sexist salutations, such as "Dear Sir."

- If you apply via email, include your cover letter as the body of the email you send so no one has to open it as an attachment.

- Don't waste the opening of your cover letter on something boring, such as "My name is…" Sell yourself. Review the sample in this chapter and explain why you are right for the job. Use the job description to help target your letter.

- The body of your letter should focus on your skills. Be as specific as possible.

- Include a call to action. Tell them what you want (an interview) and when you will follow up.

- Video cover letters are the next frontier in the career industry. Follow the advice in this chapter if you're creating a video cover letter. Most importantly: keep it short.

- Avoid mistakes. Any mistake in written correspondence will hurt your chances to land an interview.

8

Communicate Professionally Before an Interview

Communicating well at an interview requires a lot of advance preparation. Most people prepare by practicing typical interview questions, but there are a lot of other items to add to your "to do" list to help you successfully communicate during your interview. Your research should include identifying as much information about the company and the people who work there as possible, which will help you learn what to say in the interview and what questions to ask the employer.

Where to Research

Communicating well begins with research, because you'll never know what smart things you should say without learning everything you can about the employer in question. Luckily, there are a lot of places to research, and you can find most of the information you absolutely need from the comfort of your own home via your computer or mobile device.

An organization's website and social media properties

The first place to look is the most obvious. The company's website and social media streams (LinkedIn, Twitter, Facebook, Instagram, Pinterest, and any other outlets) will give you an idea of what the company values. However, don't just take the information at face value. What can you find that tells you about the company's values? Do they post about their people, or only showcase the organization? Do their employees volunteer in the community? Are they a "work hard, play hard" organization? You'll probably be able to learn a lot just from reading what they publish. Follow their social media accounts if they post there and keep up with what they're doing and what they share.

On LinkedIn, when you visit a company's page, you will be able to tell who in your network works for the organization or ties you to someone who does. Review profiles of people who work at companies that interest you. Learn about their backgrounds and skills and match your accomplishments when possible. Does everyone at a company seem to have a history working in one particular place? Perhaps that's a clue for you to start by trying to network your way into that organization as a stepping stone.

Glassdoor.com

This site collects information and reviews about companies. Keep in mind, disgruntled employees can post scathing reviews that may scare you off, so read the reviews to help guide your plans, but don't let any one review change your impression of an organization. You can find details about interviews, interview questions, and what it's like to work at the organization, including the best and worst things, on Glassdoor.com.

HOW TO COMMUNICATE THAT YOU'VE DONE YOUR RESEARCH

Don't hesitate to make it clear in an interview that you've prepared and done research. Look for opportunities to incorporate information you identified. For example, when the employer asks why you are interested in the job, you can begin your response with, "I conducted a lot of research before I decided where to apply for jobs." Go on to explain exactly what you found, and don't hesitate to mention the resources you used. You don't need to feature every resource you touched when learning about the company, but it's a good idea to make it clear that you didn't just show up for the interview. A complete answer may sound something like this:

In my research, I spent a lot of time learning about your company by reading the streams of information available via social media. I was impressed by how involved and enthusiastic so many of the employees were when talking about their work and the difference they make for their clients. I also used Hoovers to learn about the company's competitors. Based on what I learned, I believe my skills would be a good fit here.

In-Person Networking

While it's great to research online, in-person networking is a fast and easy way to learn a lot about the organization. Research networking groups in your area. Meetup.com is one resource to find groups in a variety of interest areas. Roundtown.com is another. Use the tips in chapter 1 to network and request follow-up meetings. Your goal during in-person networking is to secure one-on-one meetings with people who have information you need to help prepare for your interviews.

What to say to secure informational meetings

Keep your job-search status to yourself. If people think you're looking for a job and they don't have a job to offer, they are unlikely to agree to meet with you. Try to communicate your ability to contribute to the conversation instead of your need to seek information. For example, "I read about the new HR initiative at (organization's name) and have been interested in learning more about how it's implemented. We did something similar at my past organization, and I'd enjoy the opportunity to swap notes." If the response is, "We don't have any jobs right now," be polite, but persistent. Explain that you aren't seeking an opportunity, but only the chance to exchange information. Don't bring your resume, but do try to connect on LinkedIn and keep in touch, whether or not the individual agrees to meet you.

How to behave during an informational meeting

Most people enjoy talking about themselves, so give them plenty of opportunities to share details about their backgrounds and interests. Consider the following questions to ask:

- How did you decide to pursue this career? What is your background? (Most appropriate for entry-level inquirers.)
- What is the best thing about working at this company? What challenges are you facing? What problems are you solving right now?
- What are the most important skills needed in this organization? What are the key qualities the company seeks in hiring team members?
- Can you suggest other people for me to meet?

Exercise: Identify the information you want to know and who might be able to provide it. Start by listing five people (or job titles of people) you would like to meet. Include company names and any other details you already know. For example: Retail Buyer, Macy's, Jana Smith. List as much information as you can here to get started:

_____

_____

_____

_____

_____

_____

Before your meeting, write down what you hope to learn. If you could find out any information about the organization, what would it be? Write down some questions specific to your needs. Use the suggested questions as jumping off points to create a few questions of your own:

_____

_____

_____

_____

_____

_____

_____

_____

At these meetings, you want to offer useful, helpful information and resources. What information do you think you can provide the people you meet? What part of your background would be most useful to inspire the people you want to meet to suggest others for you to meet? Consider your resume: What successes make you most proud? What problems have you been helpful in solving? What are your best skills? Write them down here:

_____

_____

_____

_____

_____

LISTENING IS COMMUNICATING

Listening is an important part of communicating. Be an attentive and active listener during your informational meetings. Nod and smile when the other person speaks to indicate your interest. Smile and act interested in the discussion. Sit up straight and try to align your body with the other person and lean toward him or her a bit to show you're engaged. Avoid crossing your arms, which puts a barrier between you and the other person. Make consistent eye contact and don't be afraid to use your hands to punctuate your conversation. These are good rules for the informational meeting as well as for actual interviews.

After the informational meeting

Courtesy is key when communicating professionally in any circumstance, but never more than when someone shared time from his or her busy schedule to meet with you. Keep in touch by sending a prompt thank you note.

Dear [Contact]:

I want to thank you for the opportunity to speak with you on Tuesday. I was very excited to learn about your team's work. I enjoyed our conversation and appreciate your honesty about what it's like to work at [company]. I believe it would be a good fit for me in the future.

I know how busy you are, and it means a great deal to me that you took time out of your schedule to meet with me. It is clear why you've been so successful at your company.

I hope you have a great time on your trip to Alaska. I've heard the scenery is amazing, and the weather is lovely at this time of year.

Thanks for suggesting I get in touch with [insert name/s]. I will be sure to keep in touch after I hear back from them.

Sincerely,

[Your Name]

Exercise: Create a template for your thank you follow-up notes based on this sample. Fill in the information immediately after your meetings and your thank you notes will practically write themselves:

When/where was meeting?

_____

What were the key points discussed? Underline the most interesting topic or thing you learned.

_____

_____

_____

Include something relating to person's busy schedule.

_____

Include a personal item learned during meeting. (vacation, family event, or sporting event, etc.)

_____

Mention names the person provided.

_____

Note plans to keep in touch.

_____

_____

APPLY FOR THE RIGHT JOBS

Use the information you learn in your research phase for the most important step of all: be sure you apply for jobs that suit your skills and experience. Don't bother with a lot of jobs you are overqualified for, and eliminate positions if you can't prove that you have the majority of the skills they seek. This key step will help you save time in your job search, as you won't be spinning your wheels applying for positions you don't have a chance to land.

Arranging the Interview

If you live in Atlanta and get a call to interview for a job in Tampa later in the week, but no one mentions anything about travel arrangements, would you assume it's a telephone or video interview? Never assume anything regarding the details of your interviews. Always communicate about the specifics of the interview. For example, if you have an invitation to interview for a job in another city, you might respond:

I'm very interested in the XYZ position in Tampa, and I appreciate *the opportunity to discuss my qualifications with the hiring manager. I am located in Atlanta. Will this be a telephone or video interview? If we will be meeting in person, is there a budget to cover my travel expenses to meet for an in-person interview, or will I be responsible for those costs?*

Asking questions demonstrates you are detail oriented, which is an important quality for almost every job.

What to find out

- What time is the interview?
- If it is a phone appointment, is the interviewer calling you, or is it up to you to place the call?
- Does everyone have the right phone numbers?
- Who will be interviewing you? (Make sure to get the correct spellings of their names and also their contact information so you can easily follow up with thank you notes.)

When the interview is remote, it's very easy to muck up the key details, but if you are waiting for a call and the interviewer expected you to initiate the conversation, you've lost an opportunity. It's wise to send an email to confirm all the specifics so everyone is on the same page.

Items to Identify Before Your Interview

When you prepare to interview, it's tempting to believe the only way to win the job is to spend days or weeks memorizing answers for 500 possible interview questions. It's overwhelming, and luckily, it's not true. While it is a good idea to research the organization, consider potential questions the interviewer may ask, and think about how you will respond, it's a waste of time to try to memorize answers to hundreds of random questions you may never be asked.

In a blog for Glassdoor.com, Heather R. Huhman, a career and workplace expert, experienced hiring manager, and founder/president of Come Recommended, suggested keeping the following items in mind when you research for an impending interview:

1. **The company's desired skills.** Once you understand what appeals to them, you'll be in a better position to showcase those skills when you meet.

2. **Key players of the organization.** Who makes the decisions? Don't underestimate decision authority from those who might be considered lower on the office hierarchy, such as administrative assistants. Often, they have significant sway in the hiring process.

3. **News and recent events about the employer.** Don't get caught without knowing newsworthy information about an employer if you are interviewing there. Do a Google search to find out the latest news before you meet anyone in person.

4. **The company's culture, mission, and values.** Huhman quotes a Millennial Branding study that says 43 percent of HR professionals believe cultural fit is the most important quality job seekers can have during the hiring process. Make sure you understand the organization's mission and values. Once you have the information you need, you'll be able to make connections to describe why you're a good fit.

5. **Clients, products, and services.** Don't attend an interview until you really understand what the organization does and how your skills are a good match. If possible, learn as much as you can about the company's clients

and customers so you'll be able to accurately make a connection to how you can help. You should be able to articulate what products the company sells and discuss the audience (clients and customers) it serves. It's a good idea to know something about the competition and the industry, too.

6. **The person/people interviewing you.** Find out the names of the people you'll meet during an interview and Google those names beforehand. LinkedIn will be a useful resource, too. Once you learn details, such as where the person worked in the past or where they went to school, you can make connections during the interview.

Research yourself

Review your own materials carefully so you are very familiar with what they include. Review your resume and be prepared to discuss anything listed. You never know when someone will inquire about something you wrote without giving it much thought, and you don't want to be caught off guard during the interview. Evaluate your resume line-by-line and ask yourself, "What example would I give if someone asked me about this?" When you have an answer to each potential question about your skills and accomplishments, you'll be well prepared to represent yourself during interviews.

Exercise: Review your resume. Write down at least one example for each bullet point you list. For example, if you included, "Organized files and created new system to find documentation, resulting in time and money saved," your example might be in the form of a story about how an executive wanted some old information from the archives and, because of your new system, you delivered them in less than two hours when the average time might have been days or a week.

Use this space to create a checklist of information and stories of your most important accomplishments from your resume, but don't forget to review everything you've written.

_____

_____

_____

_____

_____

_____

_____

Prepare to Answer the Most Important Question

Interview preparation wouldn't be complete without at least a few practice questions. The best and most important question you should spend time preparing is the one question every interviewer will ask (in some form): "Why should I hire you?" It is the underlying question behind every other interview question. It may take many forms, for example, "What do you offer this organization?" or "Why are you the most qualified candidate?" Interviewers want to know they won't be making a mistake by hiring you.

Consider these four keys to addressing this underlying interview question:

1. Identify the connections between what the company needs and what you offer

If you're noticing a theme, you're on to something. Everything regarding your job search involves identifying the audience's interests and filling their needs. The job description is the best way to figure out what the organization wants. Study it, highlight it, and focus a lot of your attention filling in the blanks to explain why you are the person best suited to solve the organization's problems. Don't forget to read everything about the company. Consider interview preparation to be a research project. Find out everything you can and put it to use. The more you know, the better you will be able to address the underlying question, "Why should we hire you?"

2. Prepare to specifically discuss your past accomplishments as they relate to the organization's current needs

"Past performance is not indicative of future results" is a common disclaimer investment companies tell their customers. However, employers put a lot of weight in past performance. Be prepared to point out specific instances describing when you've handled the kind of problems and challenges facing the person who will fill this role. If you worked as part of a team, make sure to specify your contributions. Don't be generic in your description. Avoid saying we or the team when you're specifying your contributions. Be clear about your roles in past successes so the employer understands exactly how you can use your skills if you join his or her organization.

3. Articulate your ideas

Don't waste all of the research and information you've uncovered. Once you understand the problems facing the organization and the role you wish to fill, be prepared to talk about how you can tap your past experience to solve those problems. Employers do not spend the money to fill roles unless they have problems to solve. Do yourself and the interviewer a favor and make it clear how you might suggest addressing the issues. You'll be ahead of the majority of your competitors.

4. Incorporate your soft skills, such as attitude, communication skills, time management, and critical thinking into your answer

Otherwise known as "emotional intelligence," soft skills may make a difference between an employee who can do the job and one who does it well. Whether they admit it or not, employers want to hire candidates who are likable and easy to get along with. A recent study from Millennial Branding showed soft skills topped the list of "must have" skills that employers want, with 98 percent of employers saying communication skills are essential and 92 percent naming coordination skills.

Prepare for Phone or Video Interviews

It's not uncommon for employers to conduct interviews via phone or video, even if everyone lives in the same city. You'll want to be prepared to communicate your skills and demonstrate your strong interest in the position, even if you can't do it in person.

Video interviews

It can be a little awkward communicating via computer screen if you aren't accustomed to video conferencing or video chats. Consider the following tips to help communicate your enthusiasm to the interviewer:

- Be prepared. You won't be able to refer to your computer for any details or information, since you'll be using the screen to talk to the interviewer. Be sure you print out any documents you may need to have handy. For example, your resume, names and bios of people you're meeting, questions for the interviewer, and other details you may want to review during the conversation.

- Take a close look at the background behind you. If there is a lot of clutter, clear it up. Even if it's neat, having too much behind you can distract the interviewer. In particular, remove all personal items, especially photos. You don't want the interviewer making assumptions about you based on what he or she sees in the video window into your home or office.

- Assess the lighting situation. Make sure the area is well lit, but try to avoid too much bright light behind you.

- Make eye contact. During the interview, look directly at the camera when you're speaking. Do not look at the computer screen, because your eye contact will be awkward if you do.

- Stay still. Don't move the computer or camera around during the interview, or you may make your interviewer seasick!

- Use the same physical and non-verbal cues you would during an in-person interview. Nod your head, smile, and gesture. This will help you convey your interest and enthusiasm for the job.

Phone interviews

Phone interviews are common, so it is worth your time to think about how to prepare for them. Keep the following tips in mind, and you'll be in good shape to communicate what you have to offer during your phone interviews.

- Don't take the call from a noisy place. Your interviewer won't be impressed if you can't hear what he or she is saying because of too much noise in the background. It does not matter if the noise is your daughter's soccer game or the cappuccino machine at the local coffee shop; it's up to you to find a quiet place to take the call. If you don't, the interviewer will question your judgment, and no employer wants to hire someone who doesn't make good decisions.

- Don't forget to tell your friends and family you're on a business call. It's just your luck that someone decides to come knocking on your door the minute you get on your interview. It's distracting for you and the interviewer if you're disturbed. Be sure you alert your roommate or family members you're on an important phone call.

- Don't schedule an interview when you have other responsibilities. Never schedule an interview from your current job. Don't schedule phone interviews for times when you're responsible for children (even if you think they will be napping). If you're expecting a service person or the cable guy, they will probably come the minute you get on your call. Needless to say, don't take a phone interview during a time when you will be driving. Do yourself a favor and avoid all potential distractions so you can make a good impression.

- Don't interrupt for a call that's waiting. Just as you would never answer your phone during an in-person interview, don't ever be tempted to ask the interviewer to wait a minute so you can pick up the call that's waiting. Not only is it rude, but it's possible you'll get disconnected. When you are in an interview, give the interviewer all your focus and attention.

- Do write some notes and refer to them. Be ready for the interview. Take advantage of the fact that the interviewer can't see you and keep a few notes handy to help you remember to say all of your key points. Use bullet points, not complete paragraphs. (You don't want to read them word-for-word.)

- Be enthusiastic. In a phone interview, you need to be extra attentive about your tone and enthusiasm. If necessary, stand up when you're on the call. Smile and gesture as you would in person to help make sure you verbally project your interest in the job.

- Use a phone that won't drop the call. You do not want to lose the interviewer in the midst of your conversation. Be sure to take the call on a reliable phone in a location that isn't typically problematic.
- Listen carefully and take notes as long as it doesn't distract you. Just as it's okay to refer to your prepared notes during your interview, take advantage of the phone interview setup to write down things during the interview so you'll remember them later. It can be helpful to jot down a few things so you can write detailed thank you notes. Don't feel compelled to transcribe every word, but some well-placed notes may help you later. You'll be glad when you get the job.

Prepare Questions to Ask an Employer

One of the biggest pet peeves many hiring managers express is that interviewees are not prepared for interviews. They haven't done research about the organization and they cannot express why they are good fits for the jobs, etc. When an interviewee can ask a targeted, pointed question that gets to the root of what the hiring manager seeks, it speaks worlds for that candidate's ability to go above and beyond what is expected. Often, this "soft skill" itself is as important as any other listed ability on the job description.

Questions you should avoid

1. Do not ask anything you can easily find online. It makes you look like you're unprepared and just grasping for a question to ask. It's almost better to ask nothing than to ask something such as, "What are your most popular products?"

2. Any question that suggests you would want or need special favors. This starts when you schedule your interview.

If you start asking for special favors from the get-go, it's a red flag for employers. At the interview, don't ask about working from home or flexibility. Since schedules are usually pretty standard (either set hours or "all hours,") it's probably not helpful to ask about schedules in an interview, either.

3. Avoid asking questions that seem self-serving. For example, don't ask about benefits, vacation, or raises. That's something to address once they offer the job. Table questions about salary until it is time to negotiate.

4. Anything that makes it look like you want this job to be a stepping stone to something else. If you ask, "When could I apply for a promotion?" you're giving a clear message that you're already moving on from this job they are focused on filling. Most employers do not want to hire someone who has his eyes on the next thing. Keep your aspirations to yourself for the time being.

Ideal questions to prepare

Candidates who are really interested in the job will be inspired to do some extra research about the position and the company. Perhaps they will Google the CEO's name and see if she's said anything interesting and relevant lately that would make a good question. For example, "I noticed Fortune Magazine quoted Jane Smith as saying the company's commitment to volunteerism is one of the reasons you excel. Can you tell me more about the company's volunteer initiatives, as this is an area where I hope to contribute as an employee?"

Another approach is to make it clear you've taken time to speak to current or past employees to get a sense of the culture at the organization. For example, "I met an assistant manager who works here at a recent professional women's networking event, and she mentioned how important it is to be a team player to succeed here. Do you agree with that? How do the best teams function here?"

Start your list of questions to ask the employer with these inquiries and add your own. Remember, don't ask anything you can find out via a simple Google search or by reading the organization's website. Be smart, and don't ask questions that you can easily answer by reading the company's website. If they list their clients, for example, don't ask, "Who are your clients?"

Some possible questions to consider:

- What is expected of the new hire? What is the #1 priority for the person hired for this job?
- What are the most important skills needed for someone to be successful here?
- What are the biggest challenges facing the organization, unit, or team?
- What are the most exciting opportunities coming up that will affect this position?
- Can I meet the people who would be on the team I would join? (Don't assume you are always meeting the people you will see everyday at work.)
- What is it like to work here?

In Summary: Action Tips

- You will need to ramp up your communication skills to full force during your interview, but how well you perform will depend on your advance preparation. Include time in your busy schedule to prepare for your interviews, and you'll be much more likely to impress the employer.
- Research. Use all resources at your disposal to find out as much as possible about the employer and the job. That includes the company's website, social media properties,

interviewing people, reading the news, and checking sites such as Glassdoor.com. Make sure you incorporate useful information you find out when you speak with the employer. For example, "I read an article in The *Huffington Post* that said _____. Can you tell me more about this initiative?"

- Use informational meetings to learn new information. Review the checklists in this chapter to make the most of these opportunities. Don't forget to write a great thank you note after your informational meetings.

- Apply for the right jobs. It's so much easier to communicate your value proposition for a job when you are actually qualified for the job. Find positions that overlap with your skills.

- Be attentive to details when you're communicating about your interviews. You don't want to write down the right time, but the wrong time zone!

- Make a note of the list of things to learn before the interview. Use all of the resources at your disposal.

- Don't forget to know what YOU offer as it relates to the employer's needs. Always think of the employer first.

- Prepare and practice for the most important question: "Why should I hire you?"

- Don't forget to practice for phone and video interviews. These are as common as in-person interviews and often used for screening purposes, even for local candidates.

- Have good questions to ask at the interview. You'll look smart and impress the employer. Don't ask anything you could easily look up online.

9 Communicate Professionally During an Interview

You'll put all of your preparation to the test during your interview. There are a lot of dos and don'ts when it comes to interviewing, but when you review all of them and practice beforehand, you'll likely find most of the rules are easy to follow and only require some common sense.

Make a Good Impression

Making a good impression extends beyond simple etiquette, although a lot of your communication in an interview revolves around following basic etiquette rules. (For example, don't chew gum!) Follow these tips to ensure you communicate your interest and engagement to the employer during an interview and prove you're a great communicator.

The interview begins earlier than you think

The first thing to remember is your interview begins the minute you arrive on the employer's property. In fact, depending on your luck, it may even begin before that. Consider the story that Matt Buckland, the head of talent and recruiting for Forward Partners, told the BBC. While on the way to work, another man rudely shoved him and told him to "Go f*** yourself." As luck would have it, later that day, the rude, foul-mouthed man showed up for an interview—with Buckland. The man did not get the job, and we can easily imagine how his unfortunate behavior on the morning commute may have played a part.

While this story (made popular because Buckland tweeted about it) may be exceptional and extremely coincidental, you should behave and communicate as if you are on an interview at the very least from the moment you arrive in the parking lot or at the location of the interview. Be aware, the person you cut off in the company parking lot to grab a better parking space may be your potential boss. The woman you let the door hit on your way in the building may be your interviewer. Be sure to smile, make eye contact, and be friendly to everyone you meet on the way to your interview, and you won't face an awkward realization that you probably blew your chance at the job before you even arrived.

In particular, be sure to treat the receptionist well. Do not be rude or cavalier. Rolling your eyes or acting annoyed when asked to fill out paperwork will not stand you in good stead—body language speaks as loudly as words. Assume the receptionist's impression of you will affect your chances of landing the job. Treat everyone with respect. By the same token, don't act visibly annoyed if the interviewer keeps you waiting. Tapping your watch and shifting around loudly in your chair will not help your cause. If you believe the organization does not treat you well or the interviewer does not value your time, take it into account when evaluating the opportunity. Even if you are annoyed, maintain a polite façade. Remember, you can always decide not to accept the job offer if you don't like the way the people at the company treat you.

Be aware of your manners throughout the interview, too. For example, if you're at a lunch interview at a restaurant, and you are rude to the waiter, expect the interviewer to take notice. Say "please" and "thank you," be considerate, and don't do anything that leaves the impression that you missed important lessons about how to treat people.

Be on time

When it comes to interviews, on time means early. Plan to arrive 15–30 minutes before your interview begins, but don't go in the office until 15 minutes ahead of time. Take a test commute before the day of the interview, to get familiar with the area and know about how much time it should take you to get there.

OFFER A FIRM HANDSHAKE

Remember, people will judge you based on first impressions, and your communication begins with eye contact and a handshake. Build rapport with a great handshake. Avoid these:

- **Limp hand**—this implies disinterest and suggests you may be weak in other areas, too.
- **Fingertip handshake**—if you can't even offer your whole hand to shake, how interested are you in the job?
- **Hand pumping**—seems a little overly enthusiastic, or even aggressive.
- **Excessively tight grip**—you don't want to hurt the other person.
- **Shaking with both hands**—just use one hand for a professional handshake.

continued from page 135

Ideally, the person with the most authority in a situation (for example, the interviewer) will initiate the handshake. Be sure to stand for the handshake, and look the other person in the eye. In the United States, it's customary to hold your hand pointing toward the other person, your thumb pointing toward the ceiling. Fit your hand into the other person's hand completely. Your thumb and fingers should wrap all the way around the other person's hand. Grip firmly, but not in a Vulcan squeeze. Shake three or four times and release. Your other hand should be at your side. Some people bring their other hand around in a type of "double shake," but that's not generally appropriate in a business format.

Introduce yourself while you are shaking hands and make eye contact. "Hello, I'm Bill Smith."

Don't answer your phone

Reaching for your phone if it rings or buzzes may be such an automatic reflex, you may forget you're in an interview. It's never okay to answer or refer to your phone during an interview, so turn it off or leave it in your car.

Don't badmouth your previous boss or organization

The minute you badmouth your previous boss or employer, you tell the new employer you lack common sense. Even if your previous boss or company has a bad reputation, do not add your two cents on the matter. It's unprofessional and the employer will worry what you may say to someone about him or her down the road. Be discrete; who wants to hire a known gossip? You don't want the hiring manager to assume you would spread negative information about the new company. That would be a risk the employer is unlikely to accept. Instead, think about ways to describe past work environments in terms of what you learned or accomplishments you're proud to discuss.

Don't complain

Employers will look for subtle (and not so subtle) signs to let them know if you are a good match for their organization. Don't say anything to make it appear you are excessively negative or whiny. If you had a bad night, are really tired, hate the heat, couldn't find a parking place, or broke your heel on the way to the interview, keep it to yourself. Otherwise, you risk leaving the impression it will be unpleasant to work with you. No one likes spending time with someone who always sees the cup half empty. Smile, and don't let on if anything is bothering you.

MAINTAIN STRONG EYE CONTACT

It can be a challenge to make the perfect amount of eye contact. You don't want to stare a hole through the other person's face, but you do want to connect in a friendly, interested way. If you look away too much, you may seem shifty or not truthful, but too much eye contact can make your interviewer uncomfortable. Kara Ronin, founder of Executive Impressions, suggested the following in an article for The Muse, "Draw an imaginary inverted triangle on the other person's face around their eyes and mouth. During the conversation, change your gaze every five to 10 seconds from one point on the triangle to another." She suggests this will make you appear involved in the conversation, but without making the other person uncomfortable.

What to Say

It's easy to make a list of what you shouldn't say in an interview, but it's just as important to prepare what you will share in the interview. An alternate title for this section is, "Don't be a blabbermouth." Most people have very short attention spans. If it appears that you are going to drone on and on, your interviewer will probably begin to compose tonight's grocery list in her head rather than pay attention to your long diatribe. For example, when the interviewer asks, "Tell me about yourself," and you start with, "I was born…," you can pretty much assume you just lost your listener's attention—and probably your chance to impress the employer. Do yourself a big favor by keeping everything you say focused on information you know the employer wants to hear. Get to the point and answer the question.

Focus on your best credentials. Never lie or overinflate your qualifications. Instead, hone in on exactly what you can do as it relates to the job. If they are inviting you for an interview, they're mostly convinced you could be a good fit. As long as you were honest in your resume and application materials, you should be in good shape for the interview.

How to answer questions

This seems like obvious advice, but make sure you actually answer the question the interviewer asks. More often than not, inexperienced interviewers will get started answering a question, only to forget the actual question and instead veer off into some random story. The best way to avoid this is to use the "Problem–Action–Result" (PAR) technique to create stories and answer questions completely.

With this strategy, you'll plan ahead and be able to discuss several stories, to demonstrate you can handle any challenge the job may bring. Each story should have three elements:

1. A problem.
2. The action you took to solve the problem.
3. The result. What happened and how did your actions affect that result?

This is known as a PAR story. People who structure their responses to interview questions in this way will be sure to address all of the key points. Oftentimes, interviewees forget to describe the results of their actions, or they may forget to detail how they affected the results. When you have several PAR stories at the ready, you'll be prepared for most any interview question.

Think of times when you overcame a big challenge, worked with difficult people, or had to make an unpopular choice. These are common interview questions you can answer with a PAR story. If you research the company well, you may be able to predict some of their questions and plan some good stories to tell.

For example, if the question is, "Tell me about a time you overcame a big challenge?" You might respond:

In my current position, we report to many stakeholders. All of them have important deadlines and expect us to be able to address their concerns right away. (That's the problem.)

In order to avoid dropping any balls and not following through, and to help all of the managers who depend on us, I created a new workflow system. It includes a checklist of information and also assigns the inquiry to a particular team member. (This is the action.)

Since I've instituted the new procedures, we haven't had a single complaint, and the managing director actually called to commend our department for how well we've been able to address everyone's needs. (Result.)

What PAR stories can you use? Think about the challenges you've overcome at work and problems you've had a hand in solving. Create stories that are three or four sentences that include all of the PAR elements. The more simple the story, the better. When you have three to five such stories at your disposal, you'll be able to use them to answer just about any interview question.

Exercise: Use this space to create your PAR stories. Use this example as a template.

TOPIC: Addressing many stakeholders

Problem: All of them have important deadlines and expect us to be able to address their concerns right away.

Action: In order to avoid dropping any balls and not following through and to help all of the managers who depend on us, I created a new workflow system. It includes a checklist of information and also assigns the inquiry to a particular team member.

Result: Since I've instituted the new procedures, we haven't had a single complaint, and the managing director actually called to commend our department for how well we've been able to address everyone's needs.

TOPIC: _____

_____

Problem: _____

_____

_____

Action: _____

_____

_____

Result: _____

_____

_____

What if you don't know an answer?

It's everyone's worst interview nightmare: they ask a question and you don't know an answer. Don't panic! Stop and think for a few seconds (even if it feels like hours). Ask yourself:

- Can you use your pre-prepared problem–action–result (PAR) stories to answer the question?
- Can you tell a story that relates to the question?
- What is the intent behind the question? For example, do you think the employer wants to know about a particular skill you have?

If you still can't think of an answer, choose an aspect of the question and respond with a succinct comment—politician style. For example, perhaps the interviewer asks, "Tell me about a time you had to discipline an employee," and you can't think of a story you'd want to tell. You may say, "I'm a big believer in preventing problems with my reports before they happen. I typically address issues with employees before we have too big of a problem. This has been successful, as I have the highest retention rate of any team leaders in my company."

A "non answer" that addresses some piece of the question is better than saying, "I don't know," and some interviewers may move along and not even notice you didn't answer the question.

If the interview didn't go well, you may rely on the fact that people often remember their most recent experience of you. You may try to save a bad interview by asking really good questions at the end. A disinterested or bored interviewer may perk up if you start asking about him or her. If you Google your interviewer in advance, you may be able to come up with some good, relatable questions to help the interviewer connect with you, even if the interview didn't go as you'd like.

Even if you think you bombed the interview, send a nice thank you note and chalk it up as a learning experience.

How to respond to illegal interview questions

Unfortunately, you may encounter a few illegal (at worst) or inappropriate (at best) questions during your job search. Employers are not supposed to ask about anything related to race, gender, nationality, religious affiliation, military status, or age. However, job seekers consistently report being asked questions that address those issues. Many people involved in interviews aren't aware of the guidelines or simply ignore them. Other questions that aren't appropriate address your marital status or how many children you have (or expect to have). You have several choices when it comes to addressing these questions:

1. Answer the question. If someone asks you if you have children, you may decide to simply answer the question.

2. Refuse to answer the question. You have the right to let the employer know that you aren't required to answer the question.

3. You can examine the question for its intent and respond with an answer as it might apply to the job. For example,

if the interviewer asks, "Are you a U.S. citizen?" or "What country are you from?" you could respond, "I am authorized to work in the United States." Similarly, if the interviewer asks, "Who is going to take care of your children when you have to travel for the job?" your answer could be, "I can meet the travel and work schedule this job requires."

Keep in mind, even though questions about these topics aren't appropriate, you do learn a lot about an employer who asks them. You may decide a company that may discriminate against you based on these factors is not a place where you'd want to work.

COLLECT CONTACT INFORMATION

Be sure to collect business cards and/or other contact information from everyone you meet. This will make it easier for you to follow up with everyone after the interview is over.

Interview questions you should ask

Remember, the interview is an opportunity for you to ask your own questions of the employer. Don't miss this chance to find out information that may help you make your case for being hired and impress the interviewer.

Your goal in an interview is to demonstrate you can do the job because you have all the skills necessary to accomplish the organization's goals. When you ask good questions, it gives you a chance to delve deeper into why you are a good match. In other words, don't just ask the questions; follow up by adding a quick detail about the answer. For example, if the biggest priority is growing the client base, you'll want to mention that you expanded the client base by 25% in only three months at your past or current job.

In Chapter 8, there is a list of topics to avoid and some questions to prepare to ask at the end of an interview. Here are a few more suggestions for the day of the interview.

Ask questions that prove you've done your homework.

Employers are so relieved when candidates come to interviews well prepared and informed. Ask questions that make it clear you're informed about the organization, its goals, and its culture. It's even possible to save a bad interview by asking good questions.

- **What's the most important initiative for the person you hire in the first month?** Not only do you want to know this because it will be your job if you get this position, you'll be able to assess if the organization has any clue about what they expect this person to handle. If the reply seems too vague, overreaching, or unrealistic, you'll have the heads up that if you take the job, you could be in for a difficult start.
- **Who will be my boss and who is on the team?** Don't assume that you'll automatically meet your potential supervisor or colleagues at an interview. Make sure you have a clear understanding of who is in charge and whom you'll be relying on if you take on this position.
- **When will you be making a decision?** It's such an obvious question, but many nervous job seekers forget to find out when they can expect to hear back. This is especially important if you are the first of 30 interviews over the next three weeks, and the employer doesn't plan to be in touch before then. Instead of cooling your heels and fuming that no one is getting back to you, you can relax when you ask, "When do you expect to make an offer?" or "When will you be letting people know about the next steps in the process?"

- **What's the best way to follow up?** You don't want to annoy the interviewer with follow-up phone calls if he or she doesn't check voice mail more than once a week. Ask how to follow up and at least you'll be assured that you're getting in touch with the employer using his or her preferred methods.

What NOT to Say

While you may be comfortable and feel chatty during your interview, you'll want to keep the conversation entirely focused on what you have to offer the organization and how your accomplishments are a good match for the position opening. Some people get nervous, forget the point of the meeting, and share information they shouldn't during an interview. Keep the following topics off-limits during your job interview.

Keep your personal life to yourself

Don't over-emphasize how important your family life, social life, or hobbies are to you, even if the interviewer opens the door by mentioning his or her own family or hobbies. The point of an interview is to win the job; employers hire you for your competencies, not because you have four children or never miss your amateur soccer practice. Waxing eloquent about your family is unlikely to win favor, even in organizations with a well-known family-friendly environment. You want your potential employer to envision you being totally devoted to his or her needs.

Do not sound desperate

Perhaps you are about to default on your home or your son is about to start college, but an employer would likely consider your tenuous economic situation a negative, not a reason to hire you. Desperation is a turn-off for hiring managers. If you say, "I really need this job; or any job," the employer is likely to run the other way. Another no-no:

"I'm really flexible, I can do anything." Why is it bad to be so available? Confidence, not desperation, is the skill most employers want in a new hire. Usually, they don't go hand-in-hand; so, one whiff of "I can be anything you want me to be" or "I need this job to pay my bills" may send the employer racing in the opposite direction.

Don't complain about how hard it is to find a job

For example, don't say, "I've been having a hard time getting a job because of my age." This may or may not be true, but the potential employer doesn't care, and you're wasting your time discussing your job hunt with someone who won't hire you.

Keep your wild social life to yourself

Don't mention anything illegal, use slang or obscenities, or tell any stories about when you were drunk—even if it was ten years ago. Again, focus on the point of this meeting, which is to demonstrate that you are the best and most qualified person for the job. Don't give the interviewer any reason to doubt your professionalism.

Don't make it all about you

It can be a real turn-off to the employer when you start asking about promotions, salary, and benefits before you've sold yourself as the best candidate for the job. Asking how much vacation time you'll have, about working from home, mentioning your need to secure childcare, and requesting perks like a company car, computer, or cell phone will make the employer think you are more worried about your needs than those of the organization. This is not a selling point for you.

I'm really nervous

There's nothing wrong with feeling nervous. It's natural to be a little uneasy at an important interview. Don't tell the interviewer if you have butterflies in your stomach, though. Your job in the interview is to portray a confident and professional demeanor. You won't win any points by admitting your nerves or blaming them for any failures in your performance.

I don't really know much about the job; I thought you'd tell me all about it

It's a big mistake to come unprepared. Employers spend a lot of time interviewing, and they expect candidates to have researched the jobs enough to be able to explain why they want the positions. Otherwise, you could be wasting everyone's time by interviewing for a job you may not even really want. Asking questions is important, but don't ask anything you should know from the job description or from reading about the company online.

My biggest weakness is [something directly related to the job]

"What's your biggest weakness?" is a dreaded interview question, and you should be prepared to answer it. There's no perfect reply, but there is a reply you should never give. Never admit to a weakness that will affect your ability to get the job done. If the job description requires a lot of creativity, and you say your creativity has waned lately, assume you've taken yourself out of the running. Choose a weakness not related to the position and explain how you're working to improve it.

@#$%!

Profanity seems to be much more accepted in many workplaces today. However, an interview is not the time to demonstrate that you can talk like a pirate.

When in doubt, pause before you say what's on your mind. If you wonder if it's okay to mention something, assume it's better to avoid the topic altogether.

WORDS AND PHRASES TO AVOID USING

Jayson Demers, Founder and CEO of AudienceBloom, authored a piece for Inc.com listing words and phrases you should not use during interviews. Keep in mind, every word you say influences the employer's opinion of you. These are some he suggests you avoid. It's a good idea to keep them from all professional communication.

- **Hate.** Hate is a strong word, and if you really hate something, it's best to avoid discussing it at the interview. Instead, try to articulate your interests and feelings in a more positive way.
- **Basically.** A filler word, it doesn't have a real meaning in most cases and doesn't belong in professional conversations. What does it really mean? Did you basically solve a problem or did you actually solve it?
- **Hard working.** Saying you are hard working isn't as persuasive as demonstrating the results of your hard work. Tell a story about a time that illustrates how dedicated and hard working you are.
- **Filler words.** We all know people who include filler words in their conversations. It's difficult to make a good impression when every other word out of your mouth is *like* or *you know*. You cannot sound professional or authoritative if you incorporate a lot of these verbal ticks in your conversations. Be sure to review Chapter 13 for advice on how to avoid these filler words.

Things to Watch for During the Interview

During an in-person interview, candidates should be able to learn a lot by watching the interviewer's body language. Is he smiling and nodding? Leaning forward? Intently listening actively? If not, it may not be a good sign. If he interrupts you, rushes your answers, and seems disinterested, it's probably a sign you're not the best candidate.

If you believe the interviewer has reservations about your ability to do the job, you can ask if that is the case. If you suspect the interview isn't going well, you can try to recover after the fact with a great note articulating points you wish you had made during the conversation.

How to End the Interview

Most interviewers will give a clear sign the interview is over and ask if you have any questions. This is your opportunity to ask the questions you've prepared, along with any other topics that came up during the conversation. Your very last question should provide information about next steps in the process and timing. Especially if you believe the interview went well, you may ask, "I hope you agree I'm a good fit for the position. Based on our conversation, I believe I'd be able to make an immediate contribution. Can you tell me about next steps in the process and the timing for filling the position?"

Don't forget to ask about the best ways for you to follow up. For example, if the interviewer says the decision is about two weeks away, you may ask, "Would it be okay for me to call you in two weeks if I don't hear before then? Or, is it best to email you?" By getting permission and instruction on the best way to reach someone, you'll be ahead of the competition.

In Summary: Action Tips

- Communicating well in an interview requires some thought and preparation. When you focus on the dos and avoid the don'ts explained in this chapter, you'll be prepared to interview well.
- Make a good impression with every opportunity. This is the

time to show, not tell regarding your communication skills. Employers don't care if your resume is full of terrific skills and accomplishments if you cannot answer a question about your background succinctly.

- Assume everyone you meet on the way to your interview could be your interviewer, and act accordingly. That includes the receptionist and anyone involved in setting up your interview.
- On time really means early. There is no excuse for being late to an interview.
- Offer a firm handshake, but do not put the other person's hand in a death grip.
- Remember the things NOT to do: don't answer you phone, don't complain (about anything or anyone). Don't lie or overinflate your qualifications.
- Keep in mind what you DO want to say: focus on your best credentials as they relate to the job.
- Make good eye contact. Your body language is key when interviewing.
- Answer questions using the Problem–Action–Result (PAR) technique. Create stories and answer questions completely. Do not drone on. Keep your responses short and sweet.
- If you can't think of an answer to a question, try to fit in one of your PAR stories. If that doesn't work, try the politician's approach and respond as best you can to an aspect of the question.
- Even if the interview doesn't go well, you may be able to salvage it by asking good questions.
- Plan ahead for some questions you couldn't find answers to online.
- Collect business cards of people who interview you.
- Review the list of what not to say and what not to ask in this chapter. Focus on the questions and don't expand on your answers more than necessary.
- Always manage your body language. Don't roll your eyes or slouch.

10

Communicate Effectively After An Interview

The interview is over, so you should be able to relax now, right? Unfortunately, if you are a diligent job seeker, the work isn't over, yet. There are still important steps to take if you want to stand out from the crowd of job seekers. Follow these steps and you'll know you've done everything possible to win consideration as the best candidate for the job.

Write a Thank You Note

This is such a basic step, you'd think everyone does it. You would be wrong! Many candidates fail to take this easy, courteous step. Within 24 hours, but ideally as soon as you return home after the interview, you should have a thank you note out to the interviewer or interviewers. (Yes, you do need to write a personalized note to each person who spoke to you.)

What to write

While a basic, "Thank you for spending time speaking with me today. I appreciate your insights into the organization and willingness to answer my questions. I hope to have a chance to work together soon," is better than nothing, you can do much better (and even improve the interviewer's opinion of you) if you write a thank you note that references your discussion and specifically indicates why you are the best fit for the job.

The best thank you notes after an interview reference the specifics discussed in the interview, and ideally, even expand a bit on the topics discussed. Don't duplicate the same message to each interviewer. Comment on each meeting via individual notes to your interviewer and re-emphasize where your skills intersect with their needs and how you can solve their problems.

Your thank you notes provide opportunities to elaborate on something you want the employer to know and to remind the interviewers why you are a good choice. Remind them why you are the best person for the job and re-express your strong interest. Proofread your notes carefully for typos or errors. Recognize that by sending a note, you help yourself stand out from the rest of the candidates who do not follow through by writing a note. As long as you don't include any typos or other mistakes in your letter, sending a thank you note can only help you stand out in a crowd of candidates.

Exercise: Complete this exercise after every interview you have.

List everyone you met at the interview and include their complete contact information from their business cards.

_____

_____

_____

Write at least one key thing you discussed with that person. For example, if one interviewer seemed most interested in your accounting background, include a note about that. Is there something you did not mention when you met them that helps illustrate your qualifications for the job? Include it in your notes.

_____

_____

_____

For example:

John Jacobs, Associate Manager, XYZ Company [list address and email]
*   John was really interested in my background and experience with creating reports for government agencies. He also asked a lot of questions about specific software that I use. He was very focused on details and how important it is for this person to be detail-oriented.*

Indicate what you said when you spoke to that person.

_____

_____

_____

Is there something you forgot to say that relates to an important topic? List it.

_____

_____

_____

_____

_____

_____

Once you have your notes together for each person you met, it will be very easy to author a specific thank you note for each person. For example, the following might be a good note for John Jacobs.

Dear Mr. Jacobs:

I appreciate the opportunity to interview with you for the senior accountant position. Thank you for taking the time to answer my questions and to discuss the key qualities you are seeking for this new hire.

I was very happy to hear that one of the most important skills you hope to hire for is the ability to create effective reports for government agencies. As we discussed, detail oriented writing is a skill my supervisors consistently admire. I forgot to mention one thing related to that topic when we spoke. My boss selected me to be the head report writer for our government clients. As an extremely detail-oriented person, this is a natural fit. As we discussed, I'm also a quick study when it comes to learning new software. I am sure I would be adept at any package you choose to purchase.

Thank you again for the opportunity to interview to join your firm. I hope you'll agree I would be a natural fit for the role and look forward to hearing from you and to continuing in the process. As we discussed, if I don't hear from you by [date], I will contact your assistant.

Sincerely,

[Name]

How to send your note

Since you don't know if your contact always goes into the office (a lot of people telecommute) and since the organization may be making a quick decision, send an email thank you note right away. If you want to send something more personal to follow up after the official note, feel free; but time is of the essence, so email is a useful and quick means to deliver your note.

WHAT NOT TO SAY

Don't be labeled a "stalker" by calling and emailing your contact incessantly. If you don't hear back, assume the employer has made other arrangements and focus on different opportunities. Sara McCord, a staff writer for The Muse, compiled the following list of statements to avoid in your follow-up messages in an article for TheMuse.com.

- **You said you'd get back to me on Monday, and it's Tuesday.** No employer wants a candidate to point out the error of his or her ways in an accusing fashion. Waiting until after the appointed deadline to follow up is fine, but say something more along the lines of, "You mentioned I should touch base if I hadn't heard anything by (date)."
- **Why haven't you gotten back to me?** Clearly, employers would contact you with news. Why has it taken so long? There are any number of reasons, but none of that matters. You haven't heard yet because you haven't gotten the job,

the employer hasn't made a choice, or the whole process is put on hold.

- **I'd really appreciate any response whatsoever.** Assume the employer knows you want a reply. It's not necessary to provide a reminder.
- **I'm disappointed you never wrote me back.** It's not in your best interests to scold the employer. If you're still in the running for the position, this message probably guarantees you'll be placed on the "no thank you" list.

Once you send your thank you note, make sure you've followed all of the instructions you've received from the employer. Hopefully, you asked about next steps, so you'll know how to handle communicating with them if you don't hear anything back right away. If they said they aren't planning to make a decision for several weeks, don't be surprised if you don't hear from them. If you didn't ask about next steps, it's okay to request information via email. The key thing is to follow instructions.

Prepare for the Next Steps

If you're called back for another meeting, are you prepared for what you'll say at the higher-stakes interview? Keep on researching and preparing so you'll be ready, even if they ask you to come in the next day. Think about what you have to offer and keep the information you learned at the first interview in mind. Did the interviewer say anything that helps you learn to communicate what you offer? What about the interviewer's answers to your questions? Do they give you any clues about what to emphasize when you're called back?

Don't Put All of Your Eggs in One Basket

Even if the interview went well and you believed the hiring manager was practically offering you the job on the spot, do not stop looking for other opportunities. Unfortunately, sometimes the interviewer gave overly positive signals, and another person lands the job. Other times, the company changes course and decides to wait or freeze the position. Never count on one good interview as a promise of a job. Keep optimistic and continue to prepare, and you'll land a job sooner than if you allowed the difficult process to get you down.

Keep Your Negative Comments Offline

It's easy to find stories of people who lost job opportunities because of inappropriate posts on social media. Don't forget, if you post about your interview or ask your network if you should accept a position, expect that someone from the organization may see your updates, too. Recently, a man posted about the two jobs he was considering and asked his network which one he should accept. Unfortunately for him, one of the hiring managers saw the update and withdrew his offer.

While it's fine to post positive comments about your job search, such as, "I was thrilled to interview with a wonderful company today. I hope they have good news for me next week," it's not a good idea to write, "I couldn't believe the bozos I met at the company where I interviewed today. Plus, their salary was a total joke. No thank you." Be smart about anything you communicate via social media and expect everyone to be able to view your messages.

Keep in mind, hiring managers review social media updates, in part to learn if you have good judgment. Don't do anything to give them the impression that you'll be the type of employee they'll have to worry about down the road. Be professional if you're not offered the job, and avoid posting vituperative comments such as, "I can't believe those idiots didn't hire me. After four in-person interviews and three presentations! I can't believe I fell for their song-and-dance."

Responding to a "No"

It's not unusual for hiring managers to reconsider candidates they haven't offered jobs to in the past. If you don't land the job the first time, don't burn any bridges. Consider writing a thoughtful note to the hiring manager thanking them for considering you. Re-emphasize several of the reasons you're a great match and express your interest in being considered for future opportunities. You never know when you'll be able to turn a "no" into an offer.

In your quest to land a job, even if you missed the first opportunity, consider staying in touch with someone at the organization with whom you really connected. For example, it's a good idea to send an occasional link to an article or useful blog post. It's a good way to stay top of mind without constantly asking about opportunities.

For example:

Dear Billy Sue:

I hope you're having a great summer! Can you believe this heat? I hope you're staying cool and have an opportunity to take some time to use that beautiful sailboat.

I saw this article about new regulations affecting healthcare and thought it addressed several of the items we discussed when I interviewed for the auditor position back in March. I hope it's as interesting to you as it was to me. Numbers 2 and 4 were particularly relevant, in light of what we discussed.

I hope you'll keep in touch, and don't hesitate to let me know if there's anything I can do to help.

Sincerely,

[Your Name]

How to Accept or Decline the Position

Your dream has come true: you have an offer. It's in writing. Now, it's up to you to evaluate it and communicate your plans. Consider the following questions to ask yourself:

- How healthy are the organization's finances? Do a thorough Google search and look for business news about the organization.
- Is the location feasible, and may it change? How long is the lease for the current location, for example?
- Can you function in the organization's structure and culture?
- What do you know about your boss? Have you looked on Glassdoor.com for reviews?
- Can you fulfill the company's expectations?
- What can you expect from the company?
- How does this role help you advance your career?

Declining the offer

If you decide the job is not for you, be honest, and do not take a lot of extra time to decline the offer. A simple response, in writing, is best, but you may also call the person offering you the job before you send a note declining it. There is no need to be specific or overly detailed in your written or verbal response. Simply thank the person for the offer and decline. If you have others in mind who would be good for the job, it's okay to mention it. For example:

Thank you very much for offering the opportunity for me to join your company as the [job title]. I appreciate everything you've done to provide information to help me evaluate if the position is a good fit. I am very sorry to decline the offer. If it would be helpful, I do have several people in mind who might be great candidates and are very interested. I would be happy to forward their names to you.

Thanks again for everything you've done to assist me in this process.

Sincerely,
[Your Name]

Accepting the offer

It's a lot easier to accept the offer than it is to decline it. Again, a simple note in writing is appropriate. In this letter, you'll want to clarify key details so you have them in writing.

I am delighted to accept your offer to join XYZ company as the [job title] with a start date of [date]. I appreciate your willingness to negotiate the salary of [$ amount] and two weeks of vacation, effective immediately.

I am grateful for everything you've done to provide information to help me during this process, and I'm very excited about getting started and contributing immediately to the great team.

Thanks again for everything. I'll see you again soon.

Sincerely,

Your Name

In Summary: Action Tips

Continue to be diligent in your communications, even after the interview is over, to stand out from the crowd.

- **Write a thank you note.** Can you believe some people forget to take this basic step? Write it quickly and send it within 24 hours of your interview. Email is the best way to deliver a note, but you may want to send a follow up in writing if you are a stickler for tradition. Be sure your formal note includes specifics indicating why you are a good fit and references your conversation with the interviewer.
- **Don't overdo the communication after an interview.** You don't want to be labeled a stalker. Watch your tone and your attitude when you follow up. You don't want to offend anyone with your communication. If you've followed up according to instructions and have been diligent about following instructions, but the employer has not responded, assume they aren't interested in you and move on.
- **Always be ready for the next step.** If they invite you back for a second interview, are you ready to communicate your value proposition at the next level?
- **Be careful of what you post via social media.** Do not be a case study of what not to do online. Never post anything you wouldn't want the employer to see via your social media channels, even if you think your settings are private.
- **Don't burn bridges.** Keep communication open, even if the company sends you a rejection.
- **Use the suggestions in this chapter to evaluate offers and communicate your decisions quickly.** Dragging out your "no thank yous" isn't useful for you and may cause you problems in the future.

III ON THE JOB

CHAPTER

11

Make a Good First Impression in Person

Once you've gone through all the necessary steps to get the job, you're ready to start work. In many organizations, the first few months on the job are officially a probationary period, so it's up to you to impress from day one in order to launch yourself on the right track in your new organization. People will form opinions of you based on those early impressions. What they think of you could influence your professional career in ways you can't even imagine. Don't take these first impressions lightly.

How to Introduce Yourself

In Chapter 1, we covered how to introduce yourself in a networking environment. It's just as important to plan what to say when you meet colleagues, co-workers, and clients for the first time. "My name is…" doesn't offend anyone, but what kind of impression are you really hoping to make? What do you want them to remember about you? What do you want to be known for?

It's not all about you

Don't turn introductions into opportunities to bore people with a lot of information about yourself. Be brief, and do more listening than talking. Learn something interesting or unique about people you meet. Ask people about their hobbies and their summer plans, comment on their clothes—anything to incorporate some element into the conversation to help you identify that person later. When you make a personal or professional connection, it's easier to build a relationship. Write some notes down on the person's business card if possible, and keep reminders about their physical description, including clothing or jewelry. You may note, "Patricia: blonde curly hair, red scarf, discussed her large, unusual watch."

Consider the other person's needs

What would interest your audience most about you? Do not simply think about what you want to say; always consider his or her needs and use language that person will understand. Avoid technical jargon and don't fall into the trap of assuming someone already knows something he or she may not know—about you, your profession, or the topic of conversation.

Exercise: What is the one thing you want to be known for? Are you the best organizer this side of the Mississippi? Do you create teams that work? Do you bake a mean brownie? It's okay to include personal information in your introduction, especially when you're speaking to a group. Write down everything you hope someone will remember about you. Put a star beside the items you'd be comfortable including in your introduction.

_____

_____

_____

What to say

Consider these examples of ways to introduce yourself in various settings:

- One-on-one: Hello, Bob, it's nice to meet you. I'm Margaret. Margaret Apples, like the fruit. I just joined the IT department and look forward to re-vamping the email system.
- Group setting: Hello, everyone. My name is Abraham—Abraham Kennedy, just think of the presidents. I'm glad to be the new junior accountant. Please be sure to stop by my office, as I love to bake and usually have something sweet to share.

Repeating your first name twice gives the other person two chances to hear and to remember your name.

When you introduce yourself one-on-one, if you know the other person's name already, be sure to use it first. For example, you might start out by saying, "It's a pleasure to join you. I'm Beth; Beth Rockman, the new strategic marketing VP." Say your name slowly and articulate clearly. You may want to provide a mnemonic that makes it easier to remember your name. For example, "Bill Rogust, rhymes with August."

Body language matters

It should go without saying, but when you meet new people, do your best to project your interest and enthusiasm. Be sure to work on your eye contact, a pleasant smile, and a firm handshake. All of this will contribute to the first impression your colleagues have of you. Convey excitement via your eye contact, the tone of your voice, and your body language. Take your hands out of your pockets and avoid crossing your arms in front of you. Try to maintain an open stance so you appear welcoming and interested in meeting people. Most importantly, put down your mobile phone. When your face is buried in your phone, it's clear you're not interested in meeting new people.

A favorable impression starts with your physical stance, a smile, and a firm handshake. Stand up straight and don't slouch. Keep your stomach in, your shoulders back, and your head up. Consider where your chin is pointing. If it is facing your chest, you are probably slouching. Keep your chin tipped slightly up. Don't underestimate the importance of a smile.

Try to avoid shaking hands with sweaty palms. If you tend to have clammy hands, keep a handkerchief or small cloth to wipe your hands. Avoid a limp or weak handshake, as people will think you're not capable if you can't shake hands in a confident manner. However, there's no need to crush the other person's hand. Grip firmly, but not as if you are trying to squeeze the life out of the other person.

Don't underestimate the importance of the smile when you meet. If you grimace, look distracted, or otherwise suggest you're less than interested in meeting the other person, your reputation may forever be marred. Smile with your eyes and your mouth, and people will be more likely to remember you with a positive feeling.

Don't forget a name

Don't miss the opportunity to learn the name of each person you're meeting. Too often, people are distracted or don't pay attention during introductions and realize later they never caught the person's name. Don't let that happen to you. As you meet each new person, repeat his or her name. Instead of, "It's so nice to meet you," say, "Veronica, it's a pleasure to meet you." If, for some reason, you missed the person's name, ask for it again and then repeat it: "Miranda, that was my preschool best friend's name." Try to repeat the person's name at the beginning, middle, and end of your conversation or introduction. People like to hear their own names, so you'll win points for saying it over again.

Try to think of a way to remember your new contact's name. You may think to yourself, "Daniel, like my brother." Or, "April, like April Showers." BuildYourMemory.com suggests: "In order to remember that the name of a tall, thin man that you have just been introduced to is Mr. Adamson, you might try visualizing the biblical first man 'Adam' (complete with fig leaf), holding a little boy in his arms. Adam's son—Adamson." Another suggestion is to make an association with the name. For example, "Tall Tim" or "Handsome Harry."

Communicate to Find Success

There are several ways to easily make a good in-person impression at work beyond introducing yourself well. Consider the following ways to make a great impression on the job.

Get there early, stay late

In most cases, getting there early and staying late will help put you in good stead. When you arrive early, you'll have plenty of time to freshen up if necessary and be prepared for the day. You've heard, "The early bird gets the worm." It isn't just a trite cliché; it's a reminder that when you appear prepared and ready, you'll put yourself in a position to succeed, which helps impress your colleagues. Staying late has the same affect. Try not to bolt out the door the moment the clock strikes a certain hour. Your colleagues will notice and be favorably impressed.

Ask questions

There's never a better time to ask questions than when you start a job. Don't miss this opportunity to find out what you'll need to know to do your job well. Be careful not to ask questions that sound like you are challenging the status quo as soon as you start the job. Keep your questions to things that you are curious about and try to save the "Why do you do it that way instead of this other way?" types of inquiries for later on.

Consider the following types of questions to ask at work:

What are the biggest priorities?

If you haven't already found out the answer to this in an interview, it's a great question to ask when you begin at a job, have a new boss, or start a new project at work. Just asking the question is impressive, but following through with ideas and suggestions to help solve the problem at hand will really make a great impression.

Can I have some feedback?

While there's a lot written about how workers in the Millennial generation thrive on feedback from their supervisors, the reality is that everyone benefits from feedback in the workplace. However, it's not often a priority for organizations. This leaves some workers unsure about their contributions and status in the organization. If you want to make a good impression at work, request feedback and communication from your supervisors and colleagues. While you don't want to ask, "How am I doing?" every day, it's a good idea to open the door to feedback at work by asking for regular sit-down meetings with your supervisor.

How can I accomplish _____?

While you may be lucky and have a mentor at work, many people do not have a clear plan about their next steps at work. If you have ideas about what you'd like to do next, be sure to raise these with your boss. For example, if you've been at work for six months, and you've identified several directions you'd like to pursue, make a point to sit down with your boss to discuss them.

Exercise: It's up to you to drive your own career. Don't expect someone else to focus on you and your career if you aren't keeping up with it yourself. What are your goals and plans? Answer the following questions to help communicate your strategic work goals:

- What are your favorite parts of your job?
- Do you prefer to spend most of your time with people or alone?
- Do you aspire to manage others, or are you happy to just do your own work?
- What are your passions and interests?
- Do you want to get involved in more technical work or learn how to use new software or tools?
- Is there a specific division or department that interests you?

Take some time to think about your goals. Write down the answers to these questions so you have a reference point when you talk to your supervisor.

_____

_____

_____

_____

_____

_____

Keep in mind: During the interview process, you don't want to raise issues that are "all about you," but once you've started at a job and proven yourself to be a valuable employee, it's appropriate to consider your needs and express interest in how to steer your career in the direction you want it to go.

What are you good at, and what skills could use improvement? Bosses are impressed when you can articulate your weaknesses and suggest how you can work on them. Many organizations offer training and development, and some may even pay some part of your costs to pursue further education.

_____

_____

_____

_____

_____

_____

Do you have a dream job in mind? If so, is it a possibility at your current employer? Write down some ideas to help you move from where you are now to your dream job.

_____

_____

_____

_____

_____

_____

Are there specific people you should meet and network with? List them here. Some may be aspirational, but most people on this list should be people you can easily reach and get to know.

_____

_____

_____

_____

_____

_____

Are there skills you need to add to your repertoire? Write down your ideas about how to take steps to get where you want to go. You may need to do some research to identify the answers to these questions.

_____

_____

_____

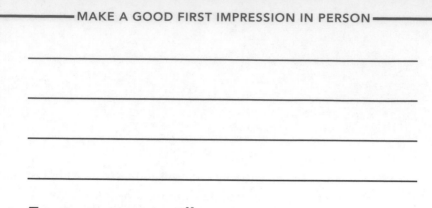

Treat everyone well

No matter what role you have at an organization, it always benefits you to treat everyone with dignity and respect. Be polite and pleasant to everyone who works with you, and you may be surprised how they are able to return the favor down the road. In many office environments, the mail people and receptionists have a lot more authority and autonomy than may be immediately evident.

Be a good listener

This deserves its own heading because you can't communicate well and make a good impression if you don't listen. If you find yourself interrupting or daydreaming when other people talk to you, it's time to step up your listening game before it negatively affects your work. Don't miss chapter 14 for more details about how to be a better listener.

SHOW GRATITUDE

An important communication tip often overlooked at work is one of the most simple and basic: say thank you. While it might be obvious that you should thank someone for a big favor, don't forget to be appreciative for the little things, too. You'll make a great impression at work by saying thank you when it's least expected. This will help you form connections with colleagues that could result in opportunities in the future.

Use stories to illustrate points

When you want to persuade or convince someone of something, or even when you just have something to share that you want people to remember, it's a good idea to use a story to prove your point. Even if your message isn't innately emotional, it can't hurt to speak to the person's emotions. Communicate personally; think about what would resonate with your audience and use that to communicate your message.

How can you paint a picture of what you want people to know? Sometimes, charts, graphs, and other visuals will do the trick. Other times, you might want to identify an analogy to demonstrate a similarity between two things. Use a simile or a metaphor. For example, "His desk was as big as a tennis court" is a simile. A metaphor example might be, "He was an unbending reed." You can see how including analogies in your speeches and writing can really bring your messages to life.

When you illustrate your points in stories that bring things into focus, you'll command more authority at work. Consider the following examples from Ken Revenaugh, innovative sales leadership consultant and trainer for CEB, on his blog FastTrackTools.com:

- The car drove past the stop sign. This person may or may not have witnessed a law being broken.
- The red car drove past the stop sign. This person has a little more detail, but the statement does not have much impact.
- The red sports car drove past the stop sign. As details build, listeners agree a law was probably broken. However, the audience doesn't really feel passionate about the situation.
- The red sports car sped past the stop sign. Now, most certainly a law was broken. The audience believes the witness and wants to act!

Vivid details help bring a story to life. Here's another example from Ken:

By printing Harry Potter and the Order of the Phoenix *on ancient forest-friendly paper, Raincoast Books minimized its impact on the environment and helped safeguard the world's ancient and endangered forests. Using 1,233 tons of 100% post-consumer recycled and processed chlorine-free paper and fiber instead of virgin fiber means that Raincoast Books is saving natural resources.*

This sounds somewhat interesting. Now, watch what happens when I give you more information about the natural resources saved by publishing this book on recycled paper using vivid equivalents:

29,640 trees = a forest area equivalent to 95 football stadiums

12,417,947 gallons of water = water filling 31 Olympic-sized swimming pools

698 tons of solid waste = 155 average female elephants

1,337 tons of greenhouse gases = a car with average fuel efficiency traveling 2.4 million miles

Clearly, adding these specifics makes the point extremely vivid!

Be Clear and Specific

Don't speak or write in generalities. Dianna Booher, author, expert on leadership communication, and founder of Booher Research, suggested several great tips about how to be specific with your colleagues for The Huffington Post.

Her examples included, "Make the person or group feel the pain of the status quo. What's doing nothing going to cost them? Loss of respect? Diminished brand? Lost productivity? Low morale? Hard dollars?" She suggests, "Paint a picture of the future if they made a change." In other words, help them visualize what you're saying.

In the same vein, Booher suggests being specific about what you say. One example she offers, "Talk about a warehouse, not a 'facility.'

Ask for an additional 'three new employees to complete the project,' not 'additional resources.'" The more specific you can be when you communicate at work, and the better you are at illustrating a visual (even if your visual is via your choice of words), the more likely your audience will be to understand your message.

Use humor carefully

It is tricky to use humor to communicate professionally. Make sure you know your audience well (and that could mean the one person you're talking to) before you introduce any humor in your communication. Don't use any humor that is at someone else's expense or makes someone the butt of a joke. This includes jokes that involve religion, sex, or ethnicities. Mike Brown, leader of The Brainzooming Group, wrote some good rules in his column for LifeHack.org. He suggests you evaluate your humor using the "SAFE" test. He suggests that all of the following should be true about what you plan to say:

- I can **S**ay/Show this to my mother.
- It wouldn't **A**nger me if I were the butt of the joke.
- This wouldn't trigger an **F**CC violation
- **E**veryone in the audience will be able to get it.

If any of these statements are not true, don't plan on sharing the humor at work.

Don't just say it, prove it

You're heard a picture is worth 1,000 words. Keep that in mind, because while what you say is important, how you act and what you do is more important. People will form an impression of you based on what you say and how you behave. Communicating well involves saying the right things, but it also means you need to act in a way that supports what you say. If you want people to believe you're a great team player, agreeing to take on team roles is one step.

Following through and actually being a team player everyone hopes will work with them requires more motivation and action. Make it your business to support your words with actions.

In Summary: Action Tips

It's not difficult to make a good impression once you know what to do and what to avoid. The best advice is to start off on the right foot and then never let your guard down.

Keep these tips in mind and you'll be able to make a strong first impression:

- **Prepare to introduce yourself at work.** Use the elevator pitch you created in chapter 1 and adapt it based on who you meet. Remember, it's not all about you. Make a connection to the other person and say something to interest him or her.
- **Find out something personal about people you meet.** This helps you make good connections later on, and if you remember what you learn, your new contacts will be very impressed with your listening skills.
- **Your body language is an important communication tool.** Stand up straight, make eye contact, smile, and offer a firm (not overly gripping) handshake.
- **Put your phone down or make sure not to take it out.**
- **Learn names.** Use the ideas in this chapter to help you remember the names of the people you meet.
- **Your impression at work extends to your behavior.** Make a good one by getting there early and staying late. Ask questions, but don't bust in and challenge the status quo the minute you arrive. Learn what you can and take advantage of your status as the new person.

- **Be kind and thoughtful to everyone in the organization.** Don't be polite to your colleagues and rude to the person who runs the mailroom. People will notice.

- **Listen when people talk.** Do not be distracted by your own concerns. You never know when you will miss something important.

- **Say thank you.** Be grateful when appropriate. This has the potential to help you stand out in a crowd of people who never stop to acknowledge another person's contribution.

- **Use rich language and stories to illustrate your points.** Paint a visual picture, even with your words, to help communicate what you want your audience to know.

- **Be clear and specific.** Don't sound wishy-washy or write in generalities. Be specific about what you need and use words that describe those needs.

- **Use humor carefully and follow Mike Brown's suggested "SAFE" test.**

- **Be who you say you are.** Hopefully, your authentic self easily conforms to these communication guidelines. If not, make it your goal to learn and follow these tips to make a great first impression.

12 Keep it Short and Sweet

Perhaps you've heard (or even said) what's become a popular phrase in some circles: "Ain't nobody got time for that." While not grammatical (and far from appropriate in most work settings), the saying does have a point. People do not have a lot of patience for much of anything these days. Social media sites like Twitter helped raise the value of short, direct messages. Short and sweet is the order of the day, and that includes work communication, both speaking and writing. How many times have you received a long memo or email that could have been truncated into one or two sentences? You wouldn't be alone if you've attended meetings that dragged on forever, but didn't seem to have any point.

You'll get ahead faster in the workplace when you tailor your communication to your audience's expectations and communicate purposefully, clearly, directly, and with intent.

Focus Your Message

Before you say or write anything at work, identify the point you want to make. Ideally, you should be able to summarize what you'd like to say in one sentence with one subject. In other words, while you could technically have a one-sentence point, creating a complex sentence with a string of commas clouds your message. What do you want people to take from your email or conversation? You can help avoid miscommunication by eliminating extraneous topics.

Think about your audience

Think about the other person's perspective. (This is a consistent theme in this book.) Communication is a two-way street. What you say or write becomes irrelevant if you couch it in layers of confusing, excess words. Avoid over-explaining and get to the point. Make the message about the person receiving it and you'll be more successful in the delivery.

Get the audience's attention

Especially when you communicate in person, be sure you attract your audience's attention before you deliver your message. It's easy to see if the other person is distracted. Make eye contact and form a connection before you make your point.

Answer the key questions

If you're confused about how to form a direct message, go back to the basics. Answer the five Ws and the H: Who, What, When, Where, Why, and How? Not every message will require a response for each of these, but they provide a guide when you're considering what you must say and what you can eliminate.

Rely on formatting

While spoken communication does not come with formatting, if you plan your messages (both in person and in writing) as if you were creating headlines and bullet points for your main topics, it will be easier to hone in on your key point. If your email or memo must be more than a few sentences, include bold headlines and subheads to help direct your reader to the main points. However, keep in mind, the longer your message, the more likely your reader will either miss key points or misinterpret what you've written.

Write Emails People Will Read

Whether or not you prefer texting or tweeting, email is still an important tool for business communication. The McKinsey Global Institute reported that the average person spends 13 hours weekly at work reading, sorting, and sending emails. How can you ensure your emails are meaningful and to the point?

Decide—do you really need to send that email?

Do you really need to add to your colleague's already clogged email inbox? Use the following criteria to help decide if an email is necessary or if a phone call or in-person visit would be better. (Be sure to review chapter 3 for a lot more tips about writing successful emails.)

Email works well in the following scenarios:

- You have a specific, concrete idea to share.
- The message is not time sensitive.
- A lot of people need to learn the exact same information.
- There are attachments to forward.
- It's difficult to reach someone by phone or in person due to schedule issues or location.
- It's important to have written proof of the communication.

Email is not the best choice under these circumstances:

- You need an answer right away.
- Nothing can be decided without a lot of back and forth communication.
- The written message could be misinterpreted easily.
- There is confidential or private information and you wouldn't want it accidentally forwarded to anyone else.
- The concepts in the email are very complicated.
- The message is emotional or highly charged.
- It would be most appropriate to deliver the message with the benefit of body language and tone.

Keep it simple

Remember to keep it focused. Stick to a single topic, if possible, and make sure it matches the subject line. If you must include more than one paragraph, bulletpoint your action items and include headlines to help break up the topics. People read a lot of their emails via mobile devices, so be sure it's easy to digest your message in a quick glance while in line at the post office or between meetings at the office. Don't bury your key message in a lot of jargon, niceties, or humor.

Pay attention to the details

Even if it's a one-paragraph email with a basic subject line, don't forget to spell check and read your message before you press "Send." Avoid silly errors, such as confusing there, their, and they're or too, two, and to. Even if the grammar police do not troll your office halls, take some pride in your writing and don't send it without at least one quick review. (Review chapter 12 for more examples of how to choose the right words in your written communication.)

Short doesn't excuse text speak

Perhaps "short and sweet" and "get to the point quickly" inspires you to want to incorporate text speak, or "txt spk" into your professional emails. While it certainly shortens your messages and may help you get to the point, it is not appropriate to use language appropriate for texting in a professional email. If you do, assume people will question your judgment.

Save your reputation

When you're writing an important message, especially a note to more than one of your colleagues, it's a good idea to compose it outside of email and then copy it into a message once you've checked it for accuracy. Another way to prevent accidentally sending an unfinished or unproofread email is to complete the "To" field after the message is fully completed. That way, no one will ever receive an accidental message from you.

Exercise: Select the best choice to complete each of the following sentences.

1. Most people in the workplace and beyond appreciate
   a. Long, detailed emails.
   b. Emails that are short and to the point.
   c. Personal, handwritten notes.
   d. None of the above.

2. Before writing anything at work
   a. Write a summary sentence of what you want to say.
   b. Ask three trusted colleagues their opinions of your proposed message.
   c. Practice in front of a mirror saying the message you want to convey.
   d. All of the above.

3. When communicating to your audience
   a. Make them repeat back to you what you've said.
   b. Think how best you can shock them with outrageous statements so they'll take notice.

c. Think what you should say so they can understand.

d. None of the above.

4. When considering how to answer a key question from an email message

    a. Ask who, what, where, when, why, and how.

    b. Google the topic and begin with lots of background information as an introduction.

    c. Use lots of short phrases and bullet points.

    d. None of the above.

5. Emails work best when

    a. You need an answer right away.

    b. A lot of back and forth communication is required.

    c. The tone is highly charged or emotional.

    d. None of the above.

6. Emails are a bad idea when

    a. You have one, concrete idea only to share.

    b. The message is not time sensitive.

    c. A lot of people need to learn the same information.

    d. None of the above.

7. Email subject lines are best when

    a. They are casual, friendly, or even vague.

    b. They take a demanding tone, such as, "Answer this immediately."

    c. They communicate importance, such as, "Time sensitive: Your input required."

    d. None of the above.

8. Email grammar and spelling are

    a. Overrated, as long as the basic message is clear, who cares?

    b. Moderately important, but only if the email goes to your superior(s).

    c. Important for making a good impression with whomever you encounter.

    d. None of the above.

9. When composing an email, it's important to

    a. Fill in the "To:" field last (to avoid accidentally sending the message before you are ready).

    b. Get your ideas on paper quickly and send it before your inner critic has a chance to sensor it, and it subsequently loses its bite.

    c. First send it to your best friend to review.

    d. All of the above.

10. Using texing abbreviations for emails is

    a. Appropriate if you are in a rush.

    b. Okay only if the recipient is a buddy.

    c. Never appropriate because it may make it difficult for recipients to understand.

    d. None of the above.

Answers

1. B

2. A

3. C

4. A

5. D

6. D

7. C

8. C

9. A

10. C

In Summary: Action Tips

Everyone is in a rush, so you need to plan your communication accordingly. Keep these tips in mind.

- **Focus your message so it is specific and concise.** If you know what you need to communicate, it will be easier to get to the point quickly before you lose the listener's attention. Answer the five Ws and the H: who, what, when, where, why, and how.

- **Always consider your audience's needs.** Communication is a two-way proposal. Make the message targeted to the other person's needs and he or she will be more interested in listening.

- **Get your audience's attention.** Is the person distracted? If it's clear you don't have the other person's attention, assume anything you say will be ignored.

- **Don't overcommunicate.** If you don't need to send an email or other communication, don't.

- **When an email is important, make sure it doesn't go unread.** Choose your subject line wisely and write something short, simple, and focused.

- **Address people appropriately and don't resort to text speak.** Hey isn't a professional salutation. Spell out your words and don't use text speak to communicate professionally. You want to be sure everyone understands what you write.

- **Proofread your emails before you send them.** Even if it's a quick message, don't forget to review it before you push "Send."

13

Say it Like You Mean It— Speak with Confidence

There is good news for professional communicators: you have a lot of control over the impression people have of you when you speak. There's also bad news: if you don't make a good impression, your colleagues may decide you're not professional, and you may lose opportunities as a result.

Speaking trouble spots aren't difficult to identify. You've heard people who can barely string a logical, understandable sentence together. Perhaps you've seen examples at your workplace. You've probably even noticed habits that detract from a speaker's credibility and those that help assign authority. Typically, if you can learn to articulate, enunciate, achieve an appropriate volume, and avoid phrasing every sentence as a question, you will demonstrate an authoritative speaking style.

Articulate Your Message and Plan Ahead

It goes without saying that your speaking style won't help you at work if your message isn't clear and people can't easily follow what you say. You can take key steps to help you sound more articulate and intelligent.

Not surprisingly, given how important research, planning, and preparation are in every other aspect of your work life, thinking ahead and organizing what you're going to say can make all the difference when you need to articulate well. Whether you're delivering a speech (when it's natural to practice and prepare) or simply making a phone call, outline your points, choose the words best suited to your audience, and practice delivering your message.

When you think about what you want to say, you're less likely to ramble, stutter, and include filler words, such as um, uh, and like. Slow down, enunciate clearly, and check your tone of voice and your body language. If you're delivering serious information, your tone and stance should match the message. Similarly, if you want someone to get back in touch with you to meet for coffee, be sure your voice and tone are upbeat and positive.

Exercise: If you have an important call to make or will be addressing your colleagues in a group setting, fill in the following chart to plan what you want to say and focus on your key points.

Point	Audience Cares About	Key Vocabulary to Include	Related Story

Watch Your Word Choice

Your audience will judge you based on your vocabulary, word choice, syntax, and grammar. Read as much as you can to enhance your vocabulary. Read magazines and online content written with an adult, sophisticated audience in mind. However, do not add unnecessarily lengthy or complex language to your everyday speech. Ideally, you'll balance your vocabulary to include impressive, well-placed language as part of a succinct, direct speaking style. With word choice, more is not better.

One way to help make yourself seem more articulate with your language is to eliminate words that make you appear less intelligent than you are. For example, avoid slang or very casual language at work. Don't ever say ya or hey, for example. Yes and hello will make you appear much more intelligent. Be sure to completely articulate your words, including the final consonant. Say want instead of wanna and going instead of goin'.

Be Politically Correct

While the term politically correct (PC) has become less about being conscious about potentially offensive behavior, and more of a term that unfortunately makes people roll their eyes, in a professional environment, it's especially important to be sensitive to others' needs. It would be unfortunate if your ill-chosen word or words offended your colleagues or potential contacts. An easy way to think about political correctness is to consider how your communication can be inclusive and welcoming to all groups of people, including those of different races, cultures, religions, genders, sexual orientations, and physical or emotional abilities. Try to avoid choosing language that would offend people who do make an effort to be inclusive in their language and communication choices. In other words, even if someone does not have a physical disability, they may still prefer you avoid using language offensive to people with physical disabilities.

A few tips to help you become more sensitive in your language choices:

- Use people-first language. In other words, instead of saying, "He's autistic," say, "The boy who has autism." Do not call someone an albino; instead, say "The girl has albinism." This emphasizes the person before the disability.

- Avoid language that elevates one religion above others. Don't assume everyone celebrates the same holidays and avoid focusing on language that mentions God or religion in your voicemail or email.
- Avoid overtly sexist language. For example, you'd never address a letter "Dear Sir." Similarly, avoid using a word such as stewardess. Flight attendant (a non gendered term) is more appropriate.
- Don't stereotype or generalize. If you use language such as "all of those people" or speak disparagingly about any group, assume you may insult someone in earshot.

Avoid Corporate Speak

If you work in a corporate environment, no doubt you hear business jargon or corporate speak on a regular basis. You're likely inspired to try to incorporate it into your own lexicon. You may want to think twice. While it's common, this type of vocabulary can be grating and annoying.

If you're looking for a mentor/advisor, consider that Richard Branson, the founder of Virgin Group and an extremely well regarded businessperson, wrote about this topic in a LinkedIn post. He said, "People love speaking in jargon, using fancy words and turning everything into acronyms." However, he recommends not using this type of language because it can confuse people. He explains, "It's far better to use a simple term and commonplace words that everyone will understand, rather than showing off and annoying your audience."

Jacqueline Smith, careers editor for Business Insider, collected a list of 26 overused business clichés in a Business Insider article. Here are a few you might want to eliminate from your communication.

- Break down the silos. What does this really mean? It refers to working together, usually across departments, where there may otherwise be barriers.
- It is what it is. Maybe this isn't difficult to understand, but it can sound negative and flip. Instead, you may want to suggest a way to change something for the better.
- Do more with less. A cliché, Smith notes, it begs the question, "Do more of what with less of what?" Say what you mean instead of relying on clichés when you speak or write.

ONLINE RESOURCES TO HELP ENHANCE YOUR VOCABULARY

- **Lingro.com.** This useful tool allows you to type a URL into its search field to turn the website you select into a clickable dictionary. Every word you choose has a pop-up dictionary definition. This works in 12 languages.
- **Visuwords.com.** This tool provides a graph to connect a word you choose to other words that are related in various ways. It allows you to hover over the words for definitions and zoom in on words that interest you.
- **Lexipedia.com.** This visual thesaurus color codes and maps out words and parts of speech. You can also see a dictionary definition of the words.
- **Thesaurus.com.** Search for any word and this tool will provide numerous other choices that mean the same thing. You can even click on each of the words for another list of potential choices. This is an easy way to spice up your language and vocabulary in writing and speaking.

Exercise: Identify Your Overused Words

Copy and paste several of your recent emails or other written correspondence into Wordle.net. The application will create a word cloud of your text, with the most often used words largest. Look at the words displayed in the largest fonts. Which of them could you easily replace with a synonym? Use the tools listed in the accompanying box to find more interesting words for the ones you tend to overuse. Your emails will immediately be more interesting and sound more intelligent.

Avoid Filler Words

Most people include filler words in their everyday speech, but some use them more than others. Try listening to yourself the next time you have to answer a question and your reply is more than a few sentences. Common fillers include so, like, uh, um, ah, I mean, like I said, and you know. You may use others not listed here. Any word or phrase that doesn't belong in a sentence and serves to give you a break or pause before you come up with the next thing you want to say is a filler word. Sometimes, we use these words to signal to people we aren't done speaking and still have more to add. Ideally, you'll eliminate all or most of these when you speak.

Exercise: Do You Use a Lot of Filler Words? Do you use a lot of fillers when you speak? It's difficult to know unless you listen to yourself. Tap into the technology you probably carry around all day long. Use a recording app (you can choose from one of the ones below or another one). Ask a friend permission to record one of your conversations and track how often you include unnecessary words. If you frequently present in front of a group, record yourself practicing the presentation and count how many times you use filler words in more formal language.

- Smart Voice Recorder (Android)
- Voice Recorder (Android)
- Voice Record Pro (iPhone)
- Recorder (iPhone)

When you use too many filler words, it may hurt your credibility and make it appear you're not very smart. Some studies suggest people may question your honesty if you hem and haw too much. It certainly will make people question your ability to communicate fluidly and capably. In addition, you'll seem ill prepared and not confident of what you are trying to say. Those are a lot of good reasons to try to avoid these when you speak.

Consider these suggestions to eliminate filler words from your language.

Prepare

When you know what you're going to say and even have a few notes written down, you can probably eliminate some of your pauses and hesitations, which often lead to using filler words. When possible, plan ahead and practice.

Pay special attention to points in a conversation when you'll be transitioning from one topic to another, as this is a prime time for filler words. If you can plan easy transitions between different topics, it will help you avoid the downtime that inevitably leads to uhms and uhs.

Avoid distractions

Focus on what you need to say. Pay no attention to what is going on in the background and you'll be less inclined to lose your train of thought. When you concentrate on what you have to say, you're less likely to rely on fillers.

Use your body language

Brett and Kate McKay wrote about this topic on Artofmanliness.com and noted that studies suggest the amount of filler words you use goes up when your arms and hands are constrained. Researchers say this may have something to do with not being able to gesture, which reduces your confidence. It can't hurt to keep your hands and arms free and see if it helps you.

Studies also suggest a lack of body language (such as when you're speaking on the phone) means some people may struggle to choose the right words to use, which may result in an uptick of fillers. Consider having more face-to-face interactions if you have a big problem eliminating fillers from your speech.

Tell a story
The McKays note that when you start to tell a story, your filler words naturally disappear. This is not really surprising, because it's easy to be engaged when telling a story that has a set beginning, middle, and end. You know what you want to say and there's no need for filler words.

Pause
Since these filler words find their way into speeches before answering a question and when transitioning from one idea to another, Steven D. Cohen, an award-winning speaker who has taught Oral Communication in the Workplace at Harvard Extension School, suggests you pause and think quietly before you answer a question. He says this technique helps you start your response powerfully and also avoid any unnecessary filler words. He offers the same advice for transition spots. Instead of trying to fill the silence, pause. Cohen's mantra is "Pause, think, answer."

Simplify your sentences
When possible, try to simplify your comments. Remember, people don't have long attention spans. No one wants to hear a long and drawn out diatribe about any topic. If you narrow down what you need to say and simplify your message, it may be easier to deliver without a lot of filler content.

Relax

It's not unusual for filler words to sneak into your speeches when you're nervous. Try to relax. Take a deep breath and remember to pause. This may help you avoid at least some of your filler words.

Pay attention

Noticing this problem is one big step toward eliminating it. Some try listening to themselves talk, and even wear rubber bands on their wrists to flick whenever they catch themselves adding fillers. Other people ask their close friends and family members to point out their speech hiccups. When you identify and focus on the problem, especially if you use these extra words frequently, it will help you solve it more quickly.

HOW TO LEAVE A PROFESSIONAL VOICEMAIL

Sometimes, a person's first impression of you will be on the phone via a voicemail. Luckily, phone calls are the easiest to prepare because you can write everything down and use your notes. Take the following steps to outline a perfect voicemail message:

- Know the person's name and how to pronounce it. If you have a hard time remembering how to say the name, write it phonetically.
- Write down what you need to tell the person. Narrow the message to the absolute basic point or points. Eliminate any extra words. Do not mention the weather or any other topic that does not relate to the reason for your call. Try to shorten the message to one or two sentences.
- Once you prepare your message, you're ready to make your call. Make sure you're in a location without background noise and where your phone will not drop the call. Don't

continued from page 198

leave professional phone messages when you're driving, for example.

- Say your name clearly and, if necessary, remind the person where you met. Speak loudly enough that it will be easy to hear you and do not mumble. Enunciate each word, but do it in a natural tone. "This is John Smith. We met at the XYZ networking event on May 7." If your name is complex and they need to know how to spell it, you can spell it for them at the end of your message.
- Deliver the message they need to know. For example: "You suggested I call to schedule a time to meet for coffee. I am free Tuesday and Thursday mornings between 10 a.m. and noon and can arrange another time with advance notice."
- Provide the information they need to respond to you and repeat your name. Please call me on my cell: 555-555-5555. It's John Smith (feel free to spell your name if necessary at this time): 555-555-5555.
- Say goodbye or provide a closing statement. "Thank you. I look forward to hearing from you."

How to Speak With Authority

When addressing an individual or a group, how you carry yourself, your body language, your tone, and your pitch make a difference in how people will perceive you. Make a point to consider all of these aspects in order to capture the authority and attention you hope to command.

Watch Your Stance

There is a lot of advice regarding how to stand to command authority. Consider the champion stance, suggested by Christine Jahnke, a speech coach and the author of *The Well-Spoken Woman*. Jenna Goudreau wrote about Jahnke's suggested stance for Forbes, noting you "position one foot in front of the other, place your weight on the back foot, hold your head up, drop your shoulders back, lean your torso slightly forward, and smile." When at a table, Jahnke advises you to put your forearms and elbows on the table while you maintain eye contact.

Whether or not you adapt the champion stance, be sure to stand up straight and do not cross your arms when you speak to people because it puts a barrier between you and appears as if you are judging them. Don't slouch or do anything to make yourself seem smaller than you are.

Eye contact

When you're talking to a group, make a point to establish eye contact with multiple people in the group. Select one person at a time and share eye contact for a sentence or two. When you speak to one person, be sure to make eye contact, but avoid locking eyes and staring, as many people will be uncomfortable. Glance to the side every five or so seconds to make a connection without causing discomfort.

Project to be heard

Most people will not assign much authority to someone with a mouse-like voice. When you sound small, your listeners will naturally treat you with less respect at work. While you do not need to speak in a booming voice, you should aim to project so you're loud enough for people to easily hear and understand what you say.

Most vocal experts advise you to improve the quality of your voice by breathing from your diaphragm. The better able you are to move air through your lungs, the louder your voice may be. Breathe in and out deeply and feel your stomach expand and contract. Try to relax your body, including your shoulders, but don't slouch or slump. This should help you naturally increase the volume of your voice.

Avoid upspeak

Do you uptalk? The habit is common, especially among women. With uptalk, or upspeak, also known more formally as High Rising Terminal (HRT), you phrase what you want to say as a question, even if it is not a question. For example, "My name is Miriam? I live in Atlanta?" Imagine my voice going up at the end, as if what I was saying was a question instead of a statement. When people include this habit in their speaking style, it may cause others to question their reliability and credibility. If everything you say sounds like a question, it's unlikely anyone will take you very seriously. Instead, they may assume you are unsure of what you are saying, or asking permission of the audience. They'll probably believe you are not sure of what you're saying. It's very difficult to command authority or attention when employing this habit, so it is something you should work on eliminating if you do this, so your statements sound declarative and not like questions.

Should you worry if you use this inflection? The Daily Mail reports on a study from Pearson that surveyed 700 people who hold managerial and executive roles. Of those surveyed, 71% agreed it was a particularly annoying trait, and 85% felt that speaking with this trait is a clear indicator of a person's insecurity or emotional weakness. Over half believed a person's professional credibility and likelihood of winning a promotion would be damaged.

As with filler words, the first step to help eliminate upspeak is to notice it's a problem with your speaking style. If you have good friends who might be willing to engage with you in eliminating this from your language, you can consider asking them to point out when you resort to this habit, either by saying something or simply making a hand gesture. If you are very aware of your behavior, it's easier to eliminate, or at least lessen how often you use this technique.

One habit that may help you avoid this behavior is beginning your key sentences with a declarative statement such as, "This is my take on it" or "I believe…" That way, it makes less sense to use upspeak, since you've set up the sentence clearly to make a statement.

If none of this works, consider recording yourself in what would otherwise be a typical work setting. You can play act with a friend and each take on a role. No matter the situation, with this technique you're likely to notice when you use this speaking crutch most often, so you can eliminate it.

Finally, if you find you're relying on upspeak because you actually do want to request feedback, try another technique instead. For example, actually ask a question, such as, "What do you think?" or "Do you agree?" Using an actual question to request feedback is a more direct way to encourage your audience's participation in the conversation without worrying that you're losing your credibility and their interest.

Use proper English and choose your words carefully

Using proper English goes a long way to gaining authority at work. Avoid slang and contractions. While not technically improper English, contractions are not ideal for written and spoken language at work. Do not sounds more formal than don't, and avoiding contractions will help make you sound more authoritative.

Keep in mind the words that affect your credibility, such as just, sort of, kind of, pretty much, maybe, really, definitely, absolutely, totally, and actually. Also, avoid overusing the pronoun I.

Don't apologize

When you apologize you imply you've done something wrong. Many people apologize in the course of typical interactions, even when there's no reason to actually be sorry. Pay attention to your speech at work. If you find yourself apologizing when you haven't done anything wrong, make a point to stop.

When you apologize in casual speech, you're asking the other person's permission to state your opinion. It makes you sound defensive and unsure of yourself, which does nothing to help make you feel and appear confident and professional.

Act confident

Even if you aren't particularly confident, if you can act as if you are, you'll be impressed by how much easier it may be to actually be confident. Don't focus on how nervous you are or on what you do not know, and your body language, eye contact, and volume should improve.

SWEARING AT WORK

If you are a newcomer to the workforce, perhaps you're surprised by how much swearing there is in your workplace. Maybe you already realized this, but sometimes, swearing does not negatively affect credibility. Forbes reported on a Northern Illinois University study by Cory R. Scherer and Brad J. Sagarin, where students listened to three speeches, and the two whose speakers cursed scored as being more persuasive than the speech without curse words.

In their study "Swearing at Work and Permissive Leadership Culture: When Anti-Social Becomes Social and Incivility Is Acceptable," researchers Yehuda Baruch and Stuart Jenkins, of the University of East Anglia in the U.K., discovered swearing at work can actually help workers bond together, improve team spirit, and form relationships. Especially if it's unexpected, swearing can win both positive and negative attention and assign the user authority, even if just for the short term.

However, each workplace is different. In cases where professionals are expected to refrain from impulsivity, cursing at work may be damaging. If your job is to appear in control at all times, randomly letting out a stream of expletives is not going to enhance your credibility or trustworthiness. Additionally, keep in mind that some will view your use of profanity as a weapon to try to dominate a situation or to aggressively seize power from more polite peers.

continued from page 203

There are also gradations of swearing, and some may be more acceptable at work than others. For example, saying sh** after spilling a glass of water on yourself is unlikely to raise many eyebrows. Cursing someone out because they've made a mistake, on the other hand, could get you in trouble, even in the most profanity-friendly workplaces.

In Summary: Action Tips

- **Practice makes perfect, and that includes practicing what you say and how you say it.** You can learn to articulate, enunciate, and demonstrate an authoritative speaking style by practicing.
- **Plan what you're going to say so you'll be prepared to be more fluid with your words.** This way, you're less likely to ramble, stutter, and include filler words such as um, uh, and like.
- **Be careful with your word choice.** Don't shorten words by dropping the last consonant, and don't use slang at work.
- **Avoid using words likely to offend other people.** Be aware of politically correct language and be inclusive when you speak.
- **Avoid corporate speak.** If you're using words that are overly jargony and don't really make sense, replace them with clearer, specific language.
- **Avoid filler words.** Use the exercises in this chapter to help avoid using them in daily speech as well as formal presentations.
- **Speak with authority by communicating confidence with your body language, including your stance and eye contact.** Be sure to project your voice so people can hear you.

- **Avoid upspeak.** Do you end every sentence with a question, even if it is not a question? You're likely undermining your authority and potentially losing out on career opportunities.
- **Don't apologize when you don't need to be sorry.** If you find yourself apologizing when you haven't done anything wrong, make a point to stop.

Pay Attention: Improve Your Listening Skills and Read Before Responding

14

When people aim to expand their communication skills, usually they think about how to improve what they say or enhance what they write. However, communication is not a one-way engagement. Your ability to *listen* when others speak and carefully *read* words on a page or screen are just as important. When you pay attention, listen, and read carefully before responding, you close the communication loop and help ensure you are truly a good communicator.

Listen and Read Carefully

"We have two ears and one mouth so we can listen twice as much as we speak." This quote, attributed to a Greek philosopher, highlights the importance of listening, which involves a lot more than simply hearing. As most people have experienced, being in the same room while someone speaks or gives instructions does not ensure strong, two-way communication. Hearing sounds is a passive activity and does not require effort on the recipient's part. Listening, on the other hand, requires focus. Active listening involves more than just hearing words; it includes attending to tone and body language and noticing when someone communicates between the lines. Ideally, the listener should appreciate verbal and non-verbal messages. In other words, if someone says she is feeling great, but speaks through clenched teeth, she's likely not so great.

Similarly, reading to understand involves a lot more than seeing words. Everyone is busy and inclined to skim to finish quickly, rather than focus to appreciate the message. In professional settings, failing to read carefully may result in responding inappropriately to emails. You don't want to be the one everyone labels inattentive to details. Especially if you know you have a tendency to lose focus, make a special effort to pay better attention to written communication at work.

WHAT IS ACTIVE LISTENING?

BusinessDictionary.com defines "active listening" as:

The act of mindfully hearing and attempting to comprehend the meaning of words spoken by another in a conversation or speech. Active listening is an important business communication skill, and it can involve making sounds that indicate attentiveness, as well as the listener giving feedback in the form of a paraphrased rendition of what has been said by the other party for their confirmation.

Active listeners aim not only to hear what is said, but also to understand the meaning behind the message and to communicate that they are involved in the conversation. They may respond periodically with verbal acknowledgements (*yes, right, hmm, uh huh*) as well as via physical indications, such as focused eye contact, nodding, and other body language, to suggest they are interested and engaged.

The Benefits of Listening Well

If you want people to pay attention when you speak, one of the most important things you can do is listen when they have something to say. While creating a checklist of what to do when you communicate (for example, project confidently) and what not to do (for example, don't use filler words and don't slouch), don't forget that active listening is a quality people admire—at work and in your personal life. If you respectfully listen to what they say, make eye contact, and respond appropriately to their concerns, they will be much more likely to give you the same respect and attention. Being a good listener is key to your professional success, as it will help you:

- **Improve your ability to make decisions and solve problems.** When you are a better listener, you are more likely to make suitable decisions. If you miss key details because you weren't paying close attention, you may make a mistake you'll regret later.
- **Learn different points of view.** Strong listeners benefit from being able to hear and understand a variety of ideas. This enhances your professional credentials.
- **Demand more respect.** When you're a good listener, you give respect, but you are also more likely to win the respect of your colleagues. This is invaluable in the workplace, where you will often need to rely on others to have your back.
- **Build better relationships.** When you are the person at work who listens well the first time and doesn't need to be told the same thing over and over again, you'll build relationships and potential referrals.
- **Become a mentor.** Being a mentor is both a responsibility and an honor. When you're known as a good listener, you're more likely to be tapped as a mentor, which can help you professionally while you help someone else.

Suggestions to Help You Become an Active Listener

If you're easily distracted, make a special effort to focus on the person, and not on his or her clothing or the surroundings. Try to push unrelated things (such as your grocery list) out of your mind and make a point to pay attention to what is being said. It could help if you purposefully nod and smile when someone speaks, if appropriate. If he or she is telling you something sad or serious, respond with body language to indicate you understand. When you react appropriately, it demonstrates you're listening.

Avoid predicting what people will say. You don't want to jump to any conclusions that may or may not be correct. Pretend to be a better listener, and it may result in you actually listening more. You may find people appreciating you and your ability to communicate with them more.

If you have a difficult time listening, consider the following tips to help you improve your ability to pay attention when someone else is speaking.

Avoid distractions

If possible, try to control the environment where you're hearing important information. If you know you're easily distracted, plan meetings in quiet places. Avoid taking directions during a lunch meeting in the cafeteria, for example. Do not, under any circumstances, reach for your phone during a conversation.

Making eye contact

It is harder to be distracted if you are really focusing on the speaker. Look at the person talking instead of out the window, at the person next to you, or something else altogether. You may be surprised by how much better a listener you become by paying close attention to eye contact.

Don't interrupt

If you're someone who is quick to want to reply to what someone else is saying, try to be slower to speak and don't feel the need to respond right away. This will help you keep your mind on what the other person is saying instead of busying your mind trying to respond.

Be attentive

Provide verbal and non-verbal queues to show you're listening. Sit still and make sure your body language shows your interest. Lean in and keep your body turned directly to the other person. Nod your head as appropriate. Your facial expression should mirror the conversation. In other words, if you're hearing a sad story, frown or shake your head sympathetically. If the person is sharing good news, smile and look excited. Verbal responses should also fit the conversation. If exclamations are appropriate (*oh, ah, I see, really?*), be sure to use them. In some cases, just a few verbal responses (um, uh huhs, or mmms) will be appropriate.

Don't be defensive

Even if you don't like what the other person is saying, or you don't agree with it, it's still important to listen and pay attention. Don't allow your distaste for what is being said prevent you from hearing the message.

Repeat information back

If you make a habit of restating or repeating important information back to someone providing instructions and asking questions, you'll hold yourself accountable and be more likely to pay attention to what's being said. In other words, you may say, "If I understand correctly, we're going to redo page one's article and focus on telling a story about accounting. My job will be to interview Bill and write a 500-word article to give you by August 30th. Does that sound right?"

Say thank you

Thanking someone for a specific piece of advice or information clearly shows you were listening and paying attention. Plus, people love to be thanked. It really helps form a connection that could result in more opportunities to share and learn.

Catch yourself when your mind wanders

When you start thinking about creating your grocery list or about what you have to do later in the day, stop yourself. Your "to do" list can wait. Push non-related thoughts from your mind to try to focus on the conversation.

Read Carefully Before Responding to Professional Correspondence

Everyone is distracted and potentially multitasking on several projects simultaneously at any given time. However, that's not an excuse to be sloppy with your written correspondence. Whether you're communicating via email, text, or another way, don't let your busy mindset prevent you from completely finishing reading information you've received.

The most important thing you can do before responding to an email or other communication is to make sure you've read it first. Do not underestimate the importance of making sure you know what's being asked of you and how other people already responded (if applicable) before you add your comments. If you fail to do so, you'll look careless (at best) and totally clueless (at worst).

Remember the lessons regarding over-copying people on emails? Don't make the email gaffes outlined in that chapter, such as replying to all or failing to include specific subject lines (or subject lines that have nothing to do with the emails below them).

In addition, don't respond right away to emails unless you have something specific to say. When you reply immediately, "I got your email and I'll get back to you," you haven't help solve any problems, and you've added one more unhelpful email to the other person's inbox.

Tips for careful reading

- If you've received a lengthy email with a lot of important details, either print it out to review (if that's a way you're better able to read it) or copy it into a document that allows you to take notes on it.
- When you read, look for words that call out action. For example, *deadline, due by,* or *respond*. Hone in on action words and make a note of anything you must do to comply or keep up.
- Be deliberate when you read work correspondence. Focus and think about what you need to do. Make notes if necessary.

Exercise: Answer **True** or **False**.

_____ **1.** Communication involves only what is said or written.

_____ **2.** Active listening is more than just hearing words.

_____ **3.** Active listeners should say *yes, right, hmm,* and, *uh huh* but not worry about eye contact and posture.

_____ **4.** Active listeners make better decisions because they pay close attention to what is said and don't miss important details.

_____ **5.** Even if you are known as a good listener, you will still be forced to demand respect from those around you.

_____ **6.** Multitasking (such as answering phone calls during a meeting with colleagues) shows you are a hard worker and instantly earns respect.

_____ **7.** Repeating back what has just been said to you is annoying and pointless.

_____**8.** Don't respond right away to emails unless you have something to say.

_____ **9.** Skimming emails is the best way to get through a mountain of correspondence.

_____ **10.** Active listening provides opportunities to hear many points of view. This enhances your professional credentials.

Answers

1. F. Communication also involves active listening, body language, and careful reading.
2. T. Hearing words is a passive activity; active listening involves attending to tone and body language. Be sure to look for and appreciate verbal and non-verbal messages.
3. F. Both eye contact and proper posture help contribute to effective listening.
4. T. Active listeners make better decisions because they pay close attention to what is said and don't miss important details.
5. F. Being a good listener is more likely to easily earn you respect.
6. F. Do not—under any circumstances—take phone calls during meetings. Multitasking is sometimes a nice word for being distracted. No one wants to feel as if they are competing for your attention.

7. **F.** Using this technique to verify what someone just said forces you to actively listen, and assures the other person that you are truly listening to what he or she said.

8. **T.** Some people may think it is more polite to immediately respond with "I got it," but clogging up someone's inbox with useless correspondence that doesn't add information is unhelpful.

9. **F.** Skimming might mean missing important information and forever being known as the team member with little attention to detail.

10. **T.** Active listening provides an opportunity to hear many points of view. This enhances your professional credentials.

In Summary: Action Tips

- Do not underestimate the importance of listening and reading carefully at work. What you say is important, but being able to pay attention well enough that you know what has been said or written for you is equally important.

- Be an active listener. Don't just hear what someone says; pay close attention and understand the meaning behind the words. Look for body language and listen for tone to be sure you understand all the key points.

- Reap the benefits of being a good listener. You have the potential to improve your ability to make decisions and solve problems. Ultimately, you'll gain respect and have the potential to build stronger relationships in all parts of your life if you're a good listener.

- Follow the tips in this chapter to become an active listener. For example, avoid distractions when you're communicating, use strong eye contact, don't interrupt or anticipate what someone might say, be attentive, and show it with your body language. Don't be defensive, but do repeat information back as a summary after a conversation, as appropriate. Say thank you, and be specific about what you appreciate. Stop yourself if your mind starts to wander and push extra thoughts away when you're listening.

- Read professional correspondence carefully before you respond. Don't be distracted and respond before you've digested the entire email or note. Read carefully and be sure you look for action words in the message, so you won't miss responding. Be deliberate and focus when you read work correspondence. Make notes if necessary.

Conclusion ▶

Professional success in our hyper-connected world depends on effective written and spoken communication. As illustrated throughout the book, strong work communication involves a lot more than being able to write a grammatical memo or ask a thoughtful question in a meeting.

Luckily, once you identify your communication deficits and evaluate how you stack up when it comes to getting your point across, you can make some relatively easy changes to improve your professional reputation. Take things step-by-step; don't get overwhelmed by the number of items you may need to improve. If you plan a strategy and follow the advice in this book, you'll be able to change how people perceive you and enhance your professional prospects.

Your success depends on many factors, including the following: creating effective job search materials, following up effectively after meetings, learning to edit your own writing and to be direct and brief in emails, and using social media effectively to showcase your expertise. It's also key to make a good impression, to apply careful reading and active listening skills to all your professional engagements, and to avoid distractions that prevent you from accessing information you need at work. Make every effort to purposely influence impressions people have of you based on what you say and write, and your professional profile will go way up.

Embrace opportunities to communicate in new ways (such as via social media) and improve in areas you may have taken for granted (such as by becoming a better listener and by following up in writing after you meet people). If you follow all of the advice included here, you'll always have your best foot forward and put yourself in the best position possible, to succeed in all of your professional situations.

Acknowledgements

"The way we communicate with others and with ourselves ultimately determines the quality of our lives." – *Tony Robbins*

Whether at work, or in your personal life, communication is key to success. With care and intention, it's not difficult to ensure your words hit their mark, improve your relationships, and expand your opportunities.

I've been fortunate to benefit from insights and information from many wonderful communicators who share content via social media. It never ceases to amaze me when a colleague shares a link to exactly the information I need at the moment. My social media stream continues to be an invaluable resource. If you haven't built your own online community, I highly recommend it.

It's a pleasure to have the opportunity to work with Sheryl Posnick, founder and president of Red Letter Content, on this, our fourth book together. Thanks for inviting me to author this manuscript, and for your editorial insights and recommendations to ensure this book is a useful tool for readers.

A special thank you to my wonderful family, including my husband, Mike, who is the best life partner I could ever want. I dedicate this book to our three boys. In a world where emotional intelligence and communication skills are increasingly crucial to success, I know each one of you will thrive.